THE
Comforts of
HOME

THE
Comforts of
HOME

Thrifty and chic decorating ideas for
making the most of what you have

Caroline Clifton-Mogg

RYLAND PETERS & SMALL
LONDON • NEW YORK

Senior designer Toni Kay
Editor Delphine Lawrance
Picture research Emily Westlake
Production Hazel Kirkman & Toby Marshall
Creative director Leslie Harrington
Cover photograph Ben Edwards

First published in 2010. This edition published
in 2023 by Ryland Peters & Small
20–21 Jockey's Fields
London WC1R 4BW
and
341 East 116th Street
New York, NY 10029

www.rylandpeters.com

10 9 8 7 6 5 4 3 2 1

ISBN 978-1-78879-498-5

A CIP record for this book is available from
the British Library.

Library of Congress CIP data has been applied for.

Printed and bound in China

FSC
www.fsc.org

MIX
Paper from
responsible sources
FSC® C106563

contents

introduction

Although 'comfort' is a word that is now often employed and used lightly, for centuries there was no such word, and when it did first appear in the English language, it was used in the sense of 'to strengthen' or 'to console'. Over time that meaning evolved to also include 'to feel at ease', and today when people say 'I feel comfortable' or 'that is comfortable', in many contexts the phrase is actually a synonym for feeling 'at home'.

Home is always important, but during uncertain times, when the wind seems to blow a little colder outside, people's thoughts often turn towards the idea of home – sometimes a specific, known place, but sometimes just a feeling; an image of somewhere that is always warm and safe, with the curtains tightly drawn against the storm outside. This home, whether real or imaginary, is not a show house – or more accurately a show-off house – but a place where material objects are less important than a sense of security and order; such qualities are intangible – they cannot be bought over a counter or bartered for – but they are hugely important in the grand scheme of things.

We should all think about the way we live, and take due care and attention as to the quality of our surroundings and the things that we live with, for care makes comfort – it cannot exist without time and effort being expended. It may seem that these are rather old–fashioned

thoughts, but it is this sort of detailed attention that makes a home comfortable and warm.

There is no doubt that the way we want to live now has changed; the idea of gross excess in all its forms is no longer desirable. Conspicuous consumption and obvious immoderation are no longer smart, while quiet enjoyment, based around the home, is seen as admirable. So perhaps this is the moment to look more closely at our homes – the places to which we return after the working day, and where we spend our leisure time – and see how we can make them more comfortable without huge injections of cash, without turning everything upside down and bringing in major changes. There are so many things that one can do to make a place, a room, more comfortable, more pleasant to be in – so many small decorative changes that rely on imagination and style rather than a deep purse; so many satisfying ways of extracting the very best out of what you already have, with comfort always firmly to the fore.

In the past, girls were taught from an early age how to run a house efficiently, often through the use of elaborate dolls' or baby houses, which were frequently made not so much for play but as three-dimensional tools to teach young girls the running of a household and where every element fitted in, how each played its part in the whole. Particularly popular in both the Netherlands and England, fine examples can still be seen in museums and books – every kitchen filled with miniature copper pans and pewter vessels, dining rooms furnished with china and glass, and four-poster beds hung with heavy embroidered curtains.

Comfort and thrift might at first seem like awkward bedfellows, but historically the two have always been linked. The smooth running of the domestic machine was the aim of all housewives – exemplified by the traditionally run country house, which for several hundred years was able to function entirely under its own steam with vegetable gardens, orchards and granaries, and designated rooms or spaces for laundry, cooking, baking and brewing, as well as a still room or workroom where tea and preserves were prepared. There were china and linen rooms, pantries and larders, where household goods and provisions were stored and treated with care and ranged in efficient order; little was discarded, but often put to new use

in a different guise. Recycling is nothing new and many of the best traditional cleaning methods are still sparklingly relevant and effective today. We can, literally, take comfort from the past – it isn't an alien country, and it does always inform the present.

Today, few of us have the luxury of unlimited space, or indeed unlimited staff, that would allow housekeeping on such a plenteous scale, but the traditional principles of good housekeeping remain the same. It is an extremely satisfying feeling to see the slatted shelves of a linen cupboard stacked with crisp, folded sheets and pillowcases, or a larder or larder cupboard filled with good, basic staples, as well as the ingredients needed to rustle up an instant, delicious supper. It is rewarding too to use textiles imaginatively, not always buying new but reviving old pieces in new contexts. All these things add to the comfort level

of our lives without necessarily incurring too much expenditure. Thinking about what makes a home comfortable is a productive exercise. The current order of the day is a house that is warm and easy to live in, decorated with individuality and taste, not excess and extravagance. Comfort and style are very easy partners, and can be quite easily achieved in a satisfying way: in general terms, for example, colour is comfortable, both on the walls and in furnishings; in particular, tablecloths, for instance, are comfortable in that they suggest delicious meals soon to be eaten. Throughout the home, from the kitchen to the bathroom, there are ways to make home life more pleasant – to refresh and rejuvenate without breaking the bank, for creating a comfortable home is actually far more about thought than money. It is also about affection – creating the comforts of home, at home, visibly demonstrates to those around you that you want them to feel at ease, and that, after all, must be a goal worth achieving.

THE ELEMENTS

The first step in creating a comfortable haven is to identify the specific aspects of home life that will most benefit from care and attention. It is important to think about how to arrange and run your home in a manner that will make everyone's life easier. Here, we examine some of the forgotten elements of a well-run household, such as the linen cupboard and the pantry, as well as how to put into practice the fine art of making the most of what you already have. It's all about finding easy ways to make your guests feel instantly, and recognizably, at home.

the joys of an orderly home

To live in the midst of disorder is disorientating, for nothing is more uncomfortable than a house where every chair is covered with old newspapers or toys, every table coated with the leftovers of the last meal, every bed unmade and every bathroom floor littered with unfolded, unhung towels.

'A real home is a self-contained place where everything works for the benefit of those who live there.'

'The easiest way to bring order into a home is to organize, and the first step in organization is to get rid of all surplus clutter.'

So why is it that in some contemporary circles the word 'order' or 'orderly' is mocked for sounding out of date and old-fashioned? Is it that their military and service connotations do not adequately convey the quiet pleasures of a home that is tidy, comfortable, friendly and warm?

A real home is a self-contained place where everything works for the benefit of the people who live there. It isn't just tidiness freaks who like to open a linen cupboard and see order – folded, stacked sheets and pillowcases instead of crumpled, billowing unidentifiable mounds. And there are few people who do not like to see an orderly pantry, well-stocked with satisfying rows of jars and bottles, tins and packets; all promising delicious meals to come.

The easiest way to bring order into a home is to organize, and the first step in organization is to get rid of all surplus clutter. I know that

everyone says to declutter, but that's because it's true. Go through room by room, starting with the kitchen: put dishes and utensils in drawers closest to where they are going to be used – tableware over the dishwasher, pots and pans near or under the cooker. Keep the work surface as clear as possible, tidying as you cook, and store things that are seldom used farthest away from the action. Use the same basic system in other rooms – think logically and all will be well.

Think logically, also, about how to clean your home. A sequential plan – cunning or otherwise – does make a big difference. Nineteenth-century manuals on housekeeping set out how to clean a house on a rota basis, suggesting not only a specific day to be assigned to a cleaning task

but also a method or system for the most efficient way to effect the cleaning – usually working from the top to the bottom of the house. Such sensible forward planning still applies, and really does cut down on what has to be done. But once you start, don't be a gadfly, stopping halfway through in order to do something else that you've just thought of. Always try and finish the task in hand before you start the next.

Occasionally, of course, when an unexpected visitation is imminent, there comes a need to slide swiftly, if temporarily, into 'Desperate Housewife' panic mode. In this instance, go straight for the visible manifestations of disorder: remove all papers from all surfaces (including chair seats), as well as any remnants of earlier snacks and drinks – from apple cores and cigarette ends to dirty plates, mugs and glasses. Do not worry about stacking the china in the dishwasher; put everything wholesale into the sink where all will be temporarily hidden. Pick up any discarded pieces of clothing – sweaters, socks and worse – and if you don't have time to deposit them in their rightful places, a nearby cupboard or even a box under a table will do for now. Fluff up seat cushions, and whisk a duster over the now clutterfree surfaces; symmetrical equates with tidy, so fold remaining papers, straighten books and put them all into neatly aligned piles.

And in the longer term, two of the most useful tips on how not to be submerged beneath chaos and to start the day feeling relaxed are to make the bed in the morning; in the evening, the psychological impact of a made bed is even greater than the cool, smooth sheets. And secondly, always, always tidy up before you go to bed.

'Think logically about how to clean your home. A sequential plan – cunning or otherwise – does make a big difference.'

making the most of what you have

Although there has always been a disparity between people who have very little and those who have too much, or at least far more than the others, today it often feels that nearly everyone has too much – or at any rate too many possessions. Too many things are jettisoned when they don't work or when they fall out of favour.

In London, on the south side of the river, is an enormous and wholly admirable recycling centre catering to the needs of four neighbouring boroughs. There, vast containers are all emptied with efficient regularity, each one holding a specific material or category, ranging from paper, garden rubbish and DVDs, to refrigerators, televisions, computers and printers. Mounds and mountains of Stuff; Stuff that a year ago was probably the apple of its owner's eye but which is now literally past its sell-by date, too old to cut the mustard with younger, newer rivals and certainly too expensive to repair.

The fact is we just have too much stuff, and today we simply discard anything that we consider no longer fit for purpose. This is the moment to change our general philosophy – to think about the pleasures of recycling and rejuvenating, and to look around at all we own, from cushions to cabinets, and think about what we can recycle, rejuvenate or learn to re-like.

Making the most of what you already have is a question of not only evaluating what is already in your house but also of appreciating it, so the first step must be to actually look at what is actually there. As with people, so with possessions – after living with them for a time, we become accustomed to their faces and sometimes no longer notice what they look like. Semi-permanent pieces of furniture, like tables and chairs, can become almost invisible; if this has happened in your house, it is time to re-evaluate – to look again at these familiar pieces, to notice where they stand and what role they play in the room. Ask yourself whether something would look better somewhere else – in another position?

'This is the moment to change our general philosophy – to think about the pleasures of recyling and rejuvenating, and to look around at all we own, from cushions to cabinets.'

Or another room even? I remember once going to an auction room with a friend on a quest for two small tables that she needed to stand either side of her bed. On returning empty-handed to her house, we thought that we would just walk round to check that there wasn't anything that she already owned that might fit the bedroom bill. There, under our very newly sharpened eyes, were two perfect tables – one hidden beneath a pile of magazines, the other almost obscured by a long curtain. The stimulus of going to the auction room to see what was available, and of then looking at what she already had with a fresh eye, gave her the ability to see, and appreciate, her own possessions in a whole new light.

In their own homes, decorators often move their furniture around on a temporary or seasonal basis, or just because they feel like it. They too like to see how things look in a new light: perhaps the sofa in front of the fire, or the chairs either side, might look better – or as good – under the window. They try things out and assess the results with a cool eye. This is a manoeuvre that has many merits and one to try at home. Moving one large piece will alter the way that everything else in the room looks; at the very worst it will show you what you can't do, and at best – and it is so much more often best than worst – it will give the room a whole new effect, as well as a completely new perspective. It may never look the same again.

Another decorator's tip, or cliché, is that nothing rejuvenates a room quicker than new cushions or lampshades. We look in detail at cushions' many merits in the section on textiles (*see pages 70-77*), but generally speaking, it is a good idea to think about changing around the cushions that you already have, for the same reasons that you move furniture – it's all too easy to get used to seeing things without seeing them. Over time, new cushions are often added to the existing stock, without any particular decorative plan. So seize the moment – pile them up and try them in other rooms, on other chairs and sofas; you may be surprised at the effect. And while thinking about how to use cushions, consider the welcoming, comfort factor of that

'It is a good idea to think about changing around the cushions that you already have – it's all too easy to get used to seeing things without seeing them.'

traditional and practical piece of seating – the deep window seat laden, naturally, with cushions. Even if you have never thought of installing one, it is worth taking a closer look at any windows that are roughly the right height from the floor to see whether a seat at windowsill level might work. It could be as simple as a bench seat or made as a box seat with a hinged top; or even as a cupboard with or without doors, where everything from odds and ends to wine bottles, with wine racks cut to fit, can be stored.

On the lamp and lampshade front, if you have table lamps, try moving some of them around onto other surfaces. Again, it might not work, but if it does, the room will look completely different

– the table lamps will bring new areas of the room into soft-lit focus, without the help of a lighting designer.

As with furniture, so with other everyday elements. When we eat at home, many of us barely ever change the way we set the table. The same mats are brought out, the same china and glass used every day at the same meals – this pattern for breakfast, these plates for supper, those tumblers and glasses at every meal. And yet most of us have several shelves of equally useful and attractive crocks that we once loved but now never use. So take them out and look at what you have: add something new to the old mix, or even change everything. Use a tablecloth instead of mats, or vice versa. It's all about trying to see the things you already have in a different, fresh light.

Practise this approach in other rooms too – with bedcovers, throws and bed linen, for example; presumably you like what you have, otherwise you wouldn't give it shelf space (and of course, if you don't like it, you could get rid of it…).

And one more tip on appreciating what you already have – nothing so sharpens the mind as seeing what other people want, and how much they might be prepared to pay for it. Go onto antique sites on the internet, graze antique price guides, look in shop windows. As the cliché goes, one man's junk is another man's treasure, and I guarantee that the moment you see an old print, chair or a vase rather like the one you have at home, the one you actually own will become even lovelier than it already is.

decorating with the senses

When you walk into a generous and well thought-out home, you can almost sense the comfort in the air. It will smell good, feel warm and look inviting. Try to use all the senses – sight, scent, hearing, taste and touch. They can, and should be used to add to the comforts of home. Use these charms discreetly however; too much of a good thing is often as unattractive as too little.

First and foremost, a comfortable home is a warm home – both physically and mentally. That doesn't mean you have to have the central heating on all day long; what it does mean is that you should conserve the heat you do have, first, as a canny friend told me, by the simple expedient of shutting the doors to every room. It seems so obvious, but the fact is that, used as we now are to working and often living in relatively open spaces with constant central heating, many of us leave connecting doors open as a matter of course.

The other obvious way that heat is lost is through the windows – up to 30% vanishes through those panes of light-bringing glass. Of course, you can add double glazing and sealants, should you so wish, but we are talking here about the comfort factor, and that comes down to curtains. If you have them, draw them at night (again, it seems obvious, but many people simply do not bother), and if you do not have them,

consider the option. Like an over-popular painter or yesterday's celebrity, curtains have seen a dramatic fall in popularity from their last heyday in the 1980s, but if comfort, warmth and cozy security are what you want, nothing beats a full pair of simple curtains, lined and interlined, and drawn snugly against the cold, winter night outside.

A house that smells lovely is instantly inviting. That doesn't have to mean expensive scented candles, although the best of them – rather than the cheap, very synthetic ones – make a house smell wonderful. Real candle aficionados sometimes use several different scented candles, each in a different room, with each separate scent complementing the last and leading the senses on. Candles apart, there are other, less perceptible ways to scent a house.

'First and foremost, a comfortable home is a warm home – both physically and mentally.'

Flowers lift the spirits, the heart and the eye; everyone loves them – even men notice a vase full of flowers. Most cut flowers and plants have their own fragile scents that do not overpower but which almost unknowingly soften the air; full-bodied blooms like lilies and roses, and gentler scents such as lilac and narcissi, all leave behind a scented impression. The sight of a flowerpot of geraniums or violets on the windowsill may be unoriginal, but is still a pleasure to the eye. Herbs in a window box or grown in pots are doubly appreciated – they look pretty, have their own clean scent and are invaluable for cooking.

There are other scents that we at once associate with a warm and comfortable home – many of which stem from memories of our childhood. These include such nostalgic smells as a large bowl of pot-pourri in a sunny room; wax-polished furniture and old leather chairs; or slow-cooking casseroles, a mound of oranges in a bowl and gently scented soap in a bathroom. Sensations such as these – you will of course have your own memory scents to add to the list – will, if you can introduce them into the home, build up layers of sensory perception and add to an overall feeling of wellbeing and ease.

Texture is important in a comfortable home: cover chairs in soft, non-scratch fabrics; have throws folded over furniture to be used as an extra layer, or simply to wrap around yourself.

And in terms of the senses, the quiet pleasures of family treasures cannot be overestimated. These are an important part of the comfortable home; they will probably not be priceless heirlooms or pieces of huge historical interest, but they will be objects and pictures that each have a story – perhaps children's books, old toys even, photographs and pictures of people from earlier generations; even board games that are traditionally played on specific occasions. They are all available – keep such things close to hand rather than hiding them away. They are individual and unique, and go a very long way towards making a house into a home.

a friendly home

A friendly home is one where everyone who enters it feels comfortable. It is, of course, what this book is about in general, but there are certain things that you can do when friends come round to make them feel glad to be with you. When people say, 'I want you to feel at home', what they mean is that they want you to feel that your surroundings feel familiar to you – even on a first visit. The way to do this is to create an atmosphere of familiarity with the physical environment and also with the sort of items within the room that might interest and amuse them as a guest.

A friendly home is, after all, one where, when people come into it, they do not feel alienated even if they have never visited your home before. It is a place where they immediately feel comfortable; physically comfortable first of all. This means a warm room and somewhere easy to sit, such as an armchair that is not piled high with old newspapers, with a table beside it at the right height, all well lit – indeed, all the things that you need in order to feel properly relaxed in your own home.

And next, the guest should be soothed, so to speak, by the surrounding attractions: speaking personally, for me the most welcoming thing to see when I come into a room – apart from a lightly chilled glass of white wine

and a comfortable chair – is a half-finished jigsaw. There is something about the sight of a jigsaw on a table that is so inviting – few can walk past without the temptation to look and see if they can find the key piece that everyone else has missed – and the very fact that it is there at all speaks volumes about the sort of companionable house they find themselves in.

Books too are an extension of the jigsaw syndrome; not only on bookshelves but also arranged in small, inviting piles on tables and surfaces around the room. They seem to invite a guest to browse through them and to relax for a moment or two – or even longer.

If you have asked your guest to eat with you, bring them to a table laid with care – that in itself shows concern for a guest's welfare and wellbeing. Use interesting china and glass, large napkins, flowers and candles – all the things that you would like to be greeted with in someone else's house. But while at a small gathering it

'If you have asked your guest to eat with you, bring them to a table laid with care – that in itself shows concern for a guest's welfare and wellbeing.'

is comparatively easy to greet each new guest and make he or she feel welcome, it is when you are holding a larger party that care must be taken to see that everyone feels immediately at home. For most people, the moment of entering a party is often the hardest part of the whole occasion – I have known many people who, upon entering a crowded, seemingly unfriendly room, have simply turned around and gone home again. And it is during the first five minutes or so that most people decide whether or not they are going to enjoy themselves.

To make certain your guests do want to stay, always ensure that you, or someone else who knows at least some of the guests, is on hand to greet everyone as they arrive. Only the most confident of souls can actually sweep with pleasure into a sea of turned backs. Secondly, do try to make sure that new arrivals are offered a drink immediately – a tray by the door

is a simple solution – for a glass in the hand is absolutely vital, both for a dose of party courage and as a social prop.

The first impression of a party room is very important, which is where lighting comes in. Many people forget about this aspect of entertaining or think that cheery bright lights are the best way for everyone to see one another and have a good time. Nothing could be less true; party lighting – whether for a large party or supper for four – should always be on the low side, and with as much candlelight as possible. Candles lend an air of interesting expectancy to any party and they also make every woman's complexion look its best.

A party is not for the host or hostess – it is for those he or she has invited, so ensure that each guest has someone to talk to, is guided and helped if necessary and is generally given a good time. That is what a friendly home is all about.

storage

Oh, the ongoing delight of having a place for everything and everything in its place! It may seem like a quiet little pleasure – certainly not one to share with the outside world – but it is a deeply satisfying, private joy nonetheless. Knowing where to look for things is, after all, the first step to finding them, and follows directly on from instilling a sense of order in the home.

'Many of the most effective forms of storage are the traditional ones – such as the pantry. Not only is the pantry traditional, it also plays a rather emotional role in the household.'

Storage must work for you in order to be effective. It doesn't matter how many drawers, shelves and cupboards there are – if they are in the wrong places or the wrong sizes, then all is for naught. So, in the same way that you have to identify what clutter you own before you can decide what to get rid of, where storage is concerned, think first about what you want to store, how and where. Happy minutes (or even hours) can be spent looking at catalogues of specialist storage equipment companies; the range of solutions for how to store everything, from tacks and screws to clothes and shoes, is unending.

The satisfaction that comes from well-arranged storage, and the thing that makes it one of the comforts of home, is the pleasure of keeping like together with like: clothes, foodstuffs, china and glass, linens, house-cleaning equipment and so on all in their right place and immediately to hand.

Surprisingly, perhaps, many of the most effective forms of storage are the traditional ones – such as the pantry. But not

only is the pantry traditional, it also plays a rather emotional role in the household. There is something about the idea of having a generous store of food, almost as a form of protection against unknown ills and dangers, and perhaps it fills an almost atavistic need to see, arranged together, cans, bottles, jars and packets – an imaginary buffer against the outside world; a source of warmth and comfort at home.

Although most of us no longer live in houses where the household's food is provided from the surrounding estate, the idea of the well-stocked pantry is still a pleasant one. You may not, of course, have room for a traditional walk-in pantry, but it's the concept that counts. So try at the very least to create a cupboard in a similar vein. The ideal pantry should be cool,

dry and without bright light. If one shelf at waist height can be made out of slate or stone, so much the better – you will be able to store cheese, butter and cold cooked meats without consigning them to the over-chilling effects of the refrigerator.

What every good pantry should contain are your regular basics, so that you don't run out of them at the wrong moment, plus a large enough variety of different foods to create a delicious meal at short notice using what you have to hand.

Cookery books often give a one-size-fits-all list of pantry essentials, but since everyone's habits and tastes are very different, I thought that I might instead list a selection of what is currently in my own pride and joy – horseshoe shelves, baskets on runners and a deep, cool granite shelf.

the perfect pantry

In wicker baskets there are:

Fresh root vegetables potatoes, onions, garlic, ginger, carrots

On the shelves above there are dried goods:

Rice Arborio, basmati, long-grain, wholemeal
Pasta spaghetti, linguine, assorted shapes
Pulses Puy lentils, split peas, black-eyed peas, chickpeas, kidney beans
Sugar caster/superfine, demarara/brown, icing/confectioners' sugar
Flour fine 00, strong white, buckwheat
Nuts and dried fruit almonds, pine nuts/kernels, chestnuts, porcini mushrooms, raisins, apricots, prunes
Salt and spices fine and sea salt, peppercorns, whole spices
Tea leaf, herbal
Stock/bouillon cubes chicken, beef, vegetable

On the next shelf is an assortment of bottles and jars:

Oils olive, corn, chilli, walnut, hazelnut
Vinegars malt, white wine, red wine, balsamic, sherry
Mustard English, French, mustard powder
Sauces ketchup, Worcestershire, brown, soya, chilli, black bean, oyster, fish
Miscellaneous essentials jams, honeys, marmalade, maple and golden (corn) syrup, coffee, drinking chocolate, cocoa, capers, gherkins, sundried tomatoes, tomato paste

And on the top shelf are cans:

Vegetables chopped and plum tomatoes, petit pois, flageolets, sweetcorn
Soup consommé, tomato, mushroom
Fish smoked mussels, smoked oysters, tuna, anchovies

'There is something incredibly soothing about looking at neat, folded piles of clean sheets and pillowcases. Wherever you keep your linen, try to divide it into type and size.'

Once you have stocked your perfect pantry, all you will need is the addition of eggs, butter, cheese and milk to make a rather good impromptu supper or two.

Another extremely traditional form of storage, as old as the pantry, is the linen cupboard; that alluring sanctum of the good housewife, which, in one's imagination, is always scented with lavender. And why not? – a lavender bag is as easy to make as tying a handkerchief together. Armoires and linen presses have been with us for hundreds of years, ever since household linens were first woven, and were used in just the same way that a linen cupboard is today, with the advantage that the contents could easily be seen through the wire-meshed doors.

Bed and table linen has always been highly admired and valued – mentioned in letters, left in wills and sewn and collected over the years for brides' trousseaux. We like linen just as much today and there is something incredibly soothing about looking at neat, folded piles of clean sheets and pillowcases, covers and spreads. Wherever you keep your linen, try to divide it into type and size, and label the shelves if possible, or subdivide the piles into drawers. The aforementioned lavender bags really do scent the linen when put on the top of the piles and slipped into the middle of stacks, as do, slightly more prosaically, used-up scent bottles.

A housekeeping cupboard does not perhaps have quite the same romantic allure as a linen cupboard or pantry, but if you can find the space to keep all your cleaning materials together, along with such necessities of life as lightbulbs, candles, tape measures, dusters and cloths, electric tape, superglue and the odd screwdriver, it does make life a lot easier, and is strangely satisfying to look into, particularly when you immediately find that odd-shaped bulb for the unusual lamp. Best of all is a cupboard large enough to fit in a dustpan and brush, vacuum cleaner, mop etc – perhaps with an ironing board hung on the inside of the door. Now that really is a cleaning cupboard!

For a long time, sewing appeared to be rather unfashionable, but needlework is beginning to be appreciated again and is fast taking its place as one of the all-time comforts of home. Few things can beat the pleasure of looking into a well-equipped, padded sewing basket. Large or small, old or new – and there are many new designs at the moment – and fitted out with different colours and weights of thread, needles in assorted sizes and weights, a pin cushion with coloured-headed pins stuck in it, a darning mushroom, thimble and tape measure, two sizes of scissors, buttons, elastic, tape and ribbon; a full sewing basket is a sight for sore eyes, and a perfect example of fit-for-purpose storage.

cleaning and care

A clean home is an essential part of a comfortable home – for although some profess not to notice, in reality there are few people who think of dirt as a pleasant or cheering thing. Clean is not a question of being obsessively so – it's more a question of not being dirty. Think how much everyone hates a dirty bath. Probably the most spine-shivering thing there is is a bath dressed with a proud, grey scumline (and don't let's even think about the shudder-making, greasy clogged-up plughole).

'Having some sort of order in a household cleaning routine can engender a feeling of calm, thanks to the pleasing sense of security that ritual and repetition can provide.'

Fresh, bright and sweet-smelling was the exhortation of old housekeeping guides, and such ideals are still just as important today. When you read one of the many contemporary descriptions of how housekeeping was tackled in previous centuries, it is evident that there was much method and organization employed. Often the week was broken up into specific tasks: traditionally, Monday was the day for washing and Tuesday for ironing; Wednesday was sewing day and Thursday for going to the market; Friday was the day to clean and Saturday to bake. Sunday, of course, was a – by then much-needed – day of rest. And tiring as it all sounds, even reading such a list does engender a certain feeling of calm – the pleasing sense of security that a certain ritual and repetition can provide, and although we may arrange things differently today, it is still necessary to have some sort of organized order in a household cleaning routine.

Of course, these days we have many labour-saving devices whereas, even by the first half of the 20th century, they had only the labour – albeit the saving – in the form of numerous servants. And although we might now be a little more jaundiced about the wonders of technology, our cleaning lives today are still a lot easier than the daily grind undertaken by the poor housemaid of even a hundred years ago.

Housemaids' duties were prescribed in household manuals of domestic manners and etiquette, such as Mrs Beeton's famous tome, the *Book of Household Management*. Isabella Beeton was herself a rather brilliant example of early marketing. Far from being, as many might imagine, a kindly old matriarch with years of home-running experience under her belt, she died in 1865 when she was only 28, having married a publisher, Samuel Beeton, nine years earlier. After her death, the canny Samuel went on updating and republishing the original book until his death in 1877 – and even then, the book carried on growing. The edition that I own was published after the First World War, still apparently under the benevolent aegis of the first household goddess, Mrs Beeton.

Even though my edition of Mrs Beeton was published in the 20th century, the work still expected of a servant in a modest household – where only cook and housemaid were kept – was prodigious. On rising, the housemaid had first to clean the kitchen, passages and kitchen stairs. Next, obviously again before breakfast could be served, came the dining room: it had to have the

rug rolled up, the table cover shaken and folded, the room swept (using tea leaves if the floor was carpet-covered), the grate cleaned, the fire lighted, the room dusted and the table laid for breakfast. And that was not all – afterwards, the poor maid had to make sure that the hall was swept, the doorsteps cleaned and the brass of the door polished. Boots and knives also needed to be cleaned before breakfast was served, which would of course have been her employers' breakfast – hers would have come later.

Other daily duties (these were over and above the regular turning out of rooms) included the dusting, tidying, sweeping and cleaning of bedrooms, the stripping and making of beds, the removal of bedroom slops and the refilling of bedroom jugs; the sweeping and cleaning of passages, stairs, drawing room, dining room and kitchen; the cleaning of silver, clearing and washing up. Before retiring she was advised to clean up the glasses and plates left over from dinner, and to prepare for her next morning's work. And so, wearily, to bed...

Of all the domestic cleaning tasks, washday has probably changed more in the last 20 years than in the previous 400; 19th-century laundering was a major undertaking and very hard work – no wonder that professional laundresses abounded to service those rich enough to afford them. In an average to large household, laundry day proceeded in an ordered and measured fashion. First of all, the water was brought to the laundry or kitchen (sometimes having to be carried from the well), and heated in tubs and vats. While the water was heating, the dirty laundry was being soaked, with the more soiled pieces rubbed

and scrubbed using a washboard and a brush – an arduous task. The clothes and linen were then immersed in hot washing tubs, where they were kept moving through the soap suds with the help of a three-legged stool or a dolly – a long wooden handle with pins or sticks on the end with which the water was agitated. It was extremely hard, physical work. When the laundry was satisfactorily cleaned, everything had to be well rinsed and whites bleached or blued (blue dye was often added as an optical brightener); all was then well starched in another tub, and then each piece was wrung through wooden rollers. After that, everything was dried – outside if you were lucky enough to have the space and good weather – and folded. Larger laundry such as bed and table linen was then put through the mangle, which rendered the linen smooth and

glossy. And last, but by no means least, everything was ironed.

This in itself was an extremely complicated task and one that required a lot of skill. One catalogue of the late 19th century describes and illustrates at least seven different designs of iron, all providing slightly different results – from the familiar flat iron that was relatively easily heated on the kitchen range, to a polishing iron with a convex, 'smooth, rounded' surface for a shiny finish, a massive box-iron with a hollow interior, into which red-hot solid pieces of metal were inserted, and even big-bellied irons heated by gas jets installed inside them. Goffering and crimping tongs for delicate frills and edgings completed the impressive arsenal.

In the same way that nowadays in the garden there is a move away from using toxic substances to grow and control plants and weeds, there is a growing movement inside the house against cleaning everything with chemical cleaners. Of course, before the overwhelming widespread use

'There is undoubtedly a feeling of slightly smug satisfaction when you create yourself something from relatively natural products that really works.'

of commercial products, most cleaning and washing products were home-made, to well-known, handed-down recipes, and many of the commercial cleaning products that we use today were designed as money-making ways of reproducing and replacing traditional home-made products, promoted for their 'convenience' factor. When these commercial cleaners were introduced, they filled a need, since it was far easier to use them than make up everything yourself; housewives began to buy these ready-bottled, labour-saving products, and home-made cleaners went out of fashion. But many cleaning products today have fairly toxic qualities, not to mention awful synthetic

smells. And while not many people would want to home-make every single cleaning product they use, there is undoubtedly a feeling of slightly smug satisfaction when you can create yourself something from relatively natural products that really works. Not only is it cheaper, sometimes substantially so, but it is also environmentally friendly and (huge advantage this) doesn't smell of what some industrial scientist and focus group manager thinks is the scent of old rose pot-pourri or – worse still – a spring morning.

Most of the 'traditional' ingredients that are now suggested for cleaning recipes are natural in the sense that they are not

manufactured, but it is interesting to see on reading old cleaning recipes that some of the ingredients used a hundred years ago would have today's health and safety police on bright red klaxon alert. It was suggested, for example, that marble be cleaned using a mixture of soft soap, quicklime and caustic potash, and a recommended method of removing stains from silver spoons was to dab them with a rag dipped in sulphuric acid. Ammonia was kept on every cleaning shelf and quicklime again, mixed with water, was often recommended as a general cleaner.

Upon studying old housekeeping manuals, it is instantly noticeable that in cleaning recipes several key ingredients continually recur; in particular,

distilled white vinegar, salt, baking soda – also known as bicarbonate of soda, or sodium bicarbonate – and borax. Like the relatively few spices needed to make a multitude of very different and delicious curries, depending on what proportions they are used in, with these few ingredients or products as the basics, a number of easy – and often extremely effective – cleaning products can be prepared. These not only work but also leave you with a glow of self-satisfaction – like the recipe for cleaning tarnished silver cutlery, whereby a sheet of aluminium foil is put loosely into a shallow dish, onto which white vinegar is poured – enough to immerse the pieces of cutlery – and a pinch of baking soda is added. The cutlery is immersed and, as you watch, the tarnish vanishes. Amazing!

Traditional cleaning methods rely on using the acid and alkaline properties of the chosen ingredient: acid cleaning agents include lemon juice, white distilled vinegar, bleach; alkaline cleaning agents include baking soda, borax,

cornmeal, soda water, cream of tartar and salt. On the next page, we have distilled, as you might say, some of the most common cleaning recipes – there are many, many others to be found, and if these work for you, experiment, and investigate. It's almost as much fun as cooking, just as rewarding and usually much easier.

During the mid-20th century, there was a sort of mini-mania for household hints – a combination, perhaps, of post-war ingenuity coupled with an ever-growing army of servantless housewives. So, from books of the period, we include here some remarkably effective examples.

'With a few ingredients or products as the basics, a number of easy and often extremely effective cleaning products can be prepared.'

random, but riveting (and untested by us):

- To prevent cakes from burning, place a shallow pan filled with salt at the bottom of the oven when baking.

- To loosen glass stoppers, pour on a little white vinegar and then turn sharply.

- To remove grass stains, rub on some treacle or molasses, then wash the garment in tepid water.

- To prevent a candle from dripping, put a little salt around the top of it before lighting.

- To make a candle fit a candlestick, dip the end in hot water – it will then be soft enough to be moulded to the necessary size.

- To clean kettles, fill them with potato parings and boil fast until quite clean.

- To make inexpensive jam or pickle covers, cut out greaseproof/wax paper to fit your jars, pour a little milk into a bowl, slip the papers into the milk and squeeze out. Spread over the jars, pressing all round; in a short time the jar will be airtight and hard, and will not need tying.

- To stitch heavy fabrics, such as duck or canvas, rub the hems and seams with soap and the needle will easily penetrate.

- To remove the smell of onions or fish from knives, stick them in a pot of earth for a time and the odour will wear off.

- To remove tea and coffee stains, soak the stained napkins and tablecloths in water in which potatoes have been boiled, then wash as normal.

things to do with baking soda

(also known as bicarbonate of soda and sodium bicarbonate):

Get rid of smells in the rubbish bin or the sink by sprinkling some baking soda in the base of the bin or on a dish to absorb them.

To clean a dirty sink, sprinkle some baking soda around the sink, leave for a few minutes, scrub lightly and rinse.

To clean silver, make a paste of three parts baking soda to one part water. Rub paste onto each piece of silver, then rinse and dry with a soft cloth.

To keep drains running freely, mix 55 g (¼ cup) baking soda with some white vinegar; leave for five minutes, then rinse with hot water.

To get rid of carpet smells, sprinkle with baking soda, leave for 15 minutes, then vacuum.

To clean lavatory bowls, sprinkle the sides of the bowl with 115 g (½ cup) baking soda, then after a few minutes pour in 125 ml (½ cup) white vinegar. Leave for 15 minutes, scrub, then flush.

things to do with white vinegar

Distilled white vinegar is a de-greaser, so it can be used in situations that involve oil and scum. As a general cleaner, mix with water and use in a spray container. 125 ml (½ cup) white vinegar with 1.2 litres (2 pints) water normally works.

To clean windows, combine 225 ml (1 cup) vinegar with 1.2 litres (2 pints) water; spray on and wipe off until dry with newspaper (which does not leave lint behind, unlike cloth).

To get rid of garlic and onion traces, wipe your hands with white vinegar after chopping.

To clean the lavatory bowl, spray neat vinegar around the bowl and brush clean.

To get rid of burned food in a pan, boil some water with white vinegar in the affected pan.

To de-scale metal kettles, boil up a solution of half vinegar, half water in the kettle.

To get rid of scorch marks on an iron, make a paste of vinegar and salt and rub onto the iron.

To get rid of cigarette or food smells, fill one or more shallow bowls with white vinegar and dot them around the affected rooms.

To get rid of red wine stains, blot a sponge with undiluted white vinegar.

things to do with borax

Borax is an alkali, so it is good for removing oily and fatty dirt. It acts as an anti-bacterial bleaching agent. Traditionally used in laundry, it has other uses too.

Laundry – for an excellent all-round laundry aid, add 115g (½ cup) to each load.

Whiten and deodorize cloth nappies/diapers by adding 115g (½ cup) borax to a bucket of warm water before dipping the nappies in.

As a stain remover on whites, make a paste of 1 tablespoon borax and 6 tablespoons water; dab on and then wash as normal.

To clean refrigerators, dissolve 1 tablespoon borax in 300 ml (½ pint) warm water and wipe down the refrigerator.

For cleaning grouting, make a paste with borax and water, then spread on the grouting; remove with a toothbrush.

textiles

If there is one element of the home that is synonymous with comfort, it is textiles. Warm and inviting, pretty and simple, they are an essential part of a room. Curtains, covers, cushions, cloths; printed and plain, in cotton and linen, silk and wool – the range and choice is so wide, it is a wonder anyone knows where to start. But since the essence of this book is about looking at what you might already have around you, or near you, and how you can use it to make your home an even warmer and more welcoming place, textiles are the perfect first stop.

I have to confess here to being something of a textile freak and I would, if I could, keep every pretty piece that came my way. As it is, I have several space-filling sets of wonderful glazed chintz curtains in storage, some dating back from windows that I dressed 30 years ago. Well, chintz must come back some time and I want to be ready when it does. I also have large remnants of every possible pattern left over from newer-made covers and curtains – after all, I may be able to use them for chair cushions and so on. Then there is the shelf crammed with bits of old textiles, including paisley and printed shawls, found in markets and antique shops – these are my absolute favourites, as every piece is unique, the colour combinations are endlessly interesting and, however you use them, they will always look different from what everybody else has.

As well as random pieces of fabric, I am particularly taken with old quilts – both plain-stitched quilts where the art is in the stitching,

which can be wonderfully elaborate, as well as every sort of patchwork and appliqué quilt. I like both European and American quilts – not only the grand ones that follow accepted traditional patterns such as Log Cabin or Flower Basket, but also the more haphazard, anything goes, designs.

So it is not surprising that I have given extensive thought to how to use, and in alternative ways, all these pieces of fabric that I like so much and would much rather see out and appreciated than languishing in a cupboard. Take quilts, for example. When I was in my quilt-buying phase, I often went to auction sales and bought job lots of two or more quilts in order to procure the one that I had earmarked for a particular bed, which left me with a lot of extra quilts. So I began to use them elsewhere – making bedroom cushions with one, and a window seat cushion with another (cutting quilts up means that you can

'Old quilts can be used to make bedroom cushions, window seat cushions or for ottoman and stool tops. The extra padding makes them very comfortable to sit on.'

use partially damaged and worn ones too) – which has been extremely successful, the extra padding making it very comfortable to sit on. The same process, using either quilts or damaged paisley shawls, can also be used for ottoman and upholstered stool tops. I used one quilt that was a bit torn, but particularly bright and cheerful, as an occasional table covering – sometimes with a smaller cloth on top; being entirely cotton, it could easily be washed on a low temperature. Another quilt I designated as an outdoor picnic rug or cloth; particularly good for this purpose are those made with an old, heavy blanket sandwiched between two layers of quilted cotton – the blanket centre acts as a barrier to damp grass, and the quilted cotton, as well as looking nicer, is cooler and far more

comfortable to sit on in the sun than a scratchy woollen rug. Folded old quilts look good at the bottom of a bed and are of course very useful as a covering for extra-cold nights.

I have also been known to buy pretty pairs of old cotton curtains when I see them. A particular pair of narrow, 19th-century printed ones that I found in Portobello Market, west London, about ten years ago languished, not unloved but certainly unused, until I acquired a flat with a window that was the right size; finally, I was able to use them – as dress curtains, with a Roman blind between – and they give me pleasure every morning. Old curtains and indeed smaller quilts can also be used just folded across the seat cushions of a sofa or chair, or hung in a panel across the back.

'The whole point of using your textiles is to show off the things that you already have, giving them a look that both amuses and pleases those who see them.'

Smaller textile pieces can also be used for upholstery – it was once quite common to use complementary combinations of colour and materials on chairs and sofas; a plain velvet perhaps for the seat with a damask or printed design for the sides and arms; and a dark cotton for the unseen back. Modern variations on this theme are endless, limited only by your own preferences, imagination and what you have to hand.

Cushions of all shapes and sizes are a first-class way of perking up a chair or sofa, and using pieces that you already have is a bonus. If it is a relatively small piece, use it on one side only, or appliqué it as a central panel over a larger piece. I also go in for instant cushion-making where I take a boring but otherwise well-made cushion, already edged with a border or braid of some sort, and having cut a piece of new fabric, sew it onto the cushion face, hemming it into the border; not only instant, but extremely satisfying.

And finally, I cannot make lampshades, but if I could I would use old, lightweight shawls or sari lengths – both being relatively translucent – and either stretch the material tightly around a frame, or attach it more loosely in a sort of old-fashioned, full-skirted way, finishing it off with braid, ribbon or even beads. For after all, the whole point of using your textiles is to show off the things that you already have, giving them a look that both amuses and pleases those who see them.

finishing touches

Personal objects – all those things that hold memories and pleasant associations – play a huge part in creating a comfortable home. Your house should be a self-contained entity, in which all the specific small details and individual touches add up to make a home. There is, after all, nothing so personal as your own collection of pictures, photographs and pieces of china, of which only you, and your family, understand the true significance; these are often the intangibles, and the way that you bring these things together and provide visual pleasure demonstrates how you like to live.

As people move through a space, they look around them. So, in your house, make the things that people are going to look at – the finishing touches – interesting and amusing; things that make the journey worthwhile.

It is lovely to go into a house and see a small collection or grouping of something treasured by the owner. I saw such a grouping recently that consisted of decorative renditions of fruit – apples and pears – each one in a different material. There was one in polished wood, another of painted plaster, a third, hand-painted porcelain and a clear glass one. They had all been arranged in a shallow bowl on a small table in the window where the light caught them, displayed to give pleasure, and looking at them, I immediately felt that pleasure. Family photographs too are pleasing to all who see them and portray some of the best features of your family life – edited by you of course!

Perhaps the most important finishing touches in a room are the pictures – a room or a house with nothing on the walls not only seems cold but actually is cold, and pictures fill that void with panache. The problem, though, comes with the way that we display them. Most of us tend to acquire pictures in a rather haphazard way, starting perhaps with a core collection and then adding new ones as and when, hanging them around the place wherever there is a space, rather than where they might be shown to best advantage. It is not that easy: all pictures look better when hung in groups or collections, and it is up to you to arrange them into compatible groups, basing your choice perhaps on subject matter or medium, size or even frame.

'Pictures look better when hung in groups or collections. Arrange them into compatible groups, basing your choice perhaps on subject matter or medium, size or even frame.'

If you can, take your pictures down from the walls, sort them into pleasing combinations and then re-hang them so that they make interesting groups – perhaps in different places, even in different rooms. There should be proportionate spaces between each frame, and each should be hung with the baseline far enough down the wall to connect with what is below. The easiest way to get this right is to arrange first your proposed group on the floor or a table, moving the pictures around until you are pleased with the result, and then either doing a rough sketch of the shapes or even taking an instant photo. By taking the time to do this properly, you will rediscover your pictures once again and take renewed enjoyment from them – as will visitors to your home.

Mirrors are often hung in the same way as pictures, and in groups with them. They can be very effective used like this, but they also have another purpose in that they can be hung in a way that almost alters the dimensions and proportions of a room, bringing light into dark corners and leading the eye from one space to another.

Closer to ground level, many finishing touches can be added that will bring even more life to the room – cushions we have already discussed, as well as objects that you like arranged on tables and other surfaces; decorative table lamps and candlesticks imply pleasant evenings ahead, and a bowl of fresh fruit is a very welcoming sight, providing colour and scent. And of course, finally, and almost most importantly, flowers – a vase, a jug, a coffee cup; branches of blossom, full bowls of garden flowers, a single tulip in a bottle – flowers tell others that yours is a home that you enjoy and that you hope they will too.

THE ROOMS

Once the elements are in place, it is time to look at the
specifics, and just as a whole is made up of its parts, the
comfortable home is made up of its different rooms. In this
section we demonstrate how every room in the house, from
the hall to the bedroom, via the kitchen and living room, can
be easily, simply and effectively rejigged and rearranged,
without too much effort or financial outlay, although quite
a lot of thought and a large injection of imagination will
possibly be required. The finished result will be worth
it – a home that is attractive, warm and friendly as well
as undeniably extremely comfortable.

THIS PAGE A dead space in a pleasingly light hall has been made into a window-cum-storage area where outdoor necessities can be easily stored. Assorted cushions and a family of oil lanterns make for a welcoming atmosphere.

ABOVE In a hall filled with natural light, a range of fresh flowers or plants add a hint of colour – displayed here in an antique wire stand.

RIGHT In a space-saving exercise in a small hall, a narrow table is placed against the staircase and over an old chest, which is used as a handy repository for hallway essentials.

the welcoming hallway

First impressions are, as we know, important (even though they are sometimes wrong), and in most would-be comfortable homes, the poor old hallway, whether in a small flat or a large country house, is the area burdened with the responsibility of conveying an impression of welcoming hospitality.

Even with a willing spirit, it is often not that easy to make a welcoming area out of a place more often concerned with being a parking lot for assorted coats and jackets, shoes, umbrellas, keys and mail. However, it can be done and the easiest way is

to visualize the hallway as a combined storage and display area; the two aspects complementing each other. The first thing to think about is the décor and lighting of the space. Obviously, a hallway must be well lit, but that does not, nor should not, mean a single, harsh overhead light. Wall sconces, dimmer switches, table lamps – a variety of sources can change the space into a room rather than a pathway.

Colour is important too. If your hallway is dark, do not automatically paint it a pale shade. Very often a rich, warm colour is more striking and conveys a welcoming impression far more effectively. Next, deal with the practicalities of the space and the storage aspect – coat stands, hooks and pegs for coats and hats; boxes, baskets or shelves for shoes, boots, gloves and scarves; drawers and at least one flat surface for keys, letters and other small objects. All these things look fine, even welcoming, as long as they have a designated place.

Once these essential elements have been taken care of, turn to the secondary aspect – the walls. Perhaps the idea of an art gallery appeals to you? In the remaining space you could group pictures closely together, leading the eye down to the rest of the house. Or create a family gallery with photographs, drawings and mementoes displayed on the wall and perhaps leaning against a narrow shelf, running the length of the space. Or even, if the space is wide enough, make a library – the walls lined with shelves for a book collection, perhaps interspersed with pictures. The important thing is that there is something in your hall to amuse or please the visitor, that lets him or her know that this is indeed a welcoming home.

ABOVE A convex mirror and decorative candle wall sconces are both attractive and functional in this hallway, while the ochre-toned walls echo the polished floorboards.

RIGHT Although this hallway corner has been designed as a practical space, this arrangement of the utilitarian in fact creates a charming, decorative composition.

THIS PAGE A hall that goes to prove that even the most disparate group of objects – some necessary, others decidedly not – can, in skilled hands, be combined to form a very pleasing group.

LEFT Comfortable wooden chairs, a scrubbed pine table top and an old dresser filled with simple china and glass make this a place in which to eat, work and just sit around.

RIGHT A range that fits into the chimney breast and a table with a pretty cloth and flowers personify the idea of kitchen comfort.

the cozy kitchen

Increasingly important in an ever faster and busier world, the kitchen, whether large or small, has become the domestic hub of every home, with comfort a priority.

We hear a lot today about 'comfort food', 'comfort eating', 'slow cooking' – now everyday phrases that all reinforce the idea that much of our domestic comfort emanates from the kitchen. The aroma of an unctuous beef casserole as you come through the door, the glimpse of a homemade cake on the table or a bowl piled high with oranges – such sights and scents are the quickest way to make everyone, both guests and family, feel immediately welcome, at home and happy. So your kitchen should always be a cozy place – not in the sense of being tiny and a little claustrophobic but rather as a friendly place; a place that exudes comfort on all levels.

What comfort on all levels means, first of all, is that the kitchen itself should be physically comfortable, whether it is

BELOW This kitchen, with no highfalutin desires for modernity or new technology, is simply a pleasant, functional and comfortable room that has been fit for purpose for many years.

RIGHT More than in any other room, a mixture of traditional shapes and patterns will always work well in the kitchen, no matter how modern the overall design.

FAR RIGHT This kitchen is a clever blend of modern technology and traditional design that combines different materials, particularly wood and ceramic, to comfortable and immediate effect.

conceived in traditional or contemporary style. Taking its obvious function into account, it should be a well-designed environment where the preparation and cooking of food is easy and stressfree; where kitchen life is a pleasure, not a chore. It should be an area in which it is easy to work and to move about; a cozy kitchen is not one where you trip up on piles of pans and plates, nor one where you need a satellite navigation system to negotiate a route through the chaos. It is instead one with a place for everything and with everything in its place.

In design terms, the kitchen has – not exactly imperceptibly, but certainly without much obvious fanfare – moved on. When the first all-modern, shiny fitted kitchens were introduced in the mid-20th century, they were generally not considered to be public rooms: they were very definitely places where meals were prepared, if not in secret, then certainly behind almost closed doors, to be produced, in their entirety, at the

THIS PAGE Every housewife's dream – a kitchen large enough to have everything within easy reach. Open shelves mean that the decorative and the functional can be accessed at all times.

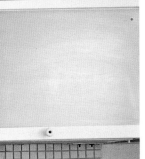

appointed hour. But times and lifestyles have changed, and as living patterns have become less formal, so the kitchen has begun to assume an ever more important and central role in the home, and is now often planned and designed either as part of a larger eating and living area or situated adjacent to and opening into a separate eating space. This means that the traditional, ergonomically efficient kitchen layout, the kitchen triangle – where cooking, washing and refrigeration areas are positioned at the points of an imaginary triangle – is now developing into a less rigid space. The kitchen contains more flexible work zones where different areas have various interdependent functions and are linked, both practically and decoratively, to the other parts of the room.

The rise in popularity of the island unit, for example, is testimony to this desire for more flexibility in the kitchen layout. In the modern comfortable kitchen, an island unit, with its characteristically wide countertop (one side operating as a work surface, the other as a bar), can act as a link between the practical and social aspects of today's kitchen. A refinement of the basic design is a split-level countertop, with one side raised so that guests can sit and chat to the

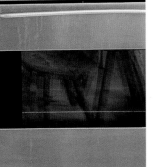

ABOVE RIGHT A most basic but utterly practical kitchen with utensils hung from a metal bar and storage concealed behind striped curtains slotted onto expanding wire.

RIGHT Even a mini kitchen under the attic eaves can be both efficient and cozy, as long as thought is given to providing ample storage for all necessary foodstuffs and equipment.

ABOVE A small kitchen has been made into a family room full of welcome. The walls are decorated with children's artwork and colour is brought in with the chair seats, table mats and kitchenware.

ABOVE RIGHT When you have pretty things in the kitchen, rather than keeping them hidden away, leave them on display where they can be enjoyed. They are sure to warm up your surroundings.

FAR RIGHT There is something intrinsically satisfying about kitchen utensils. When they are arranged with thought on open shelves, they make an eye-pleasing and idiosyncratic display.

cook, the other lower and equipped with perhaps a stove, an extra sink and a food preparation area.

If you have a large kitchen, a table for lounging at, as well as for eating at, is a magnet for the family and a real comfort-inducing element. And if you do have a table, make sure that the accompanying chairs – as well as any extra chairs scattered around the room – are comfortable enough for someone to read in as well as to talk.

The materials used to create a comfortable kitchen are important, and as far as comfort seekers are concerned, whether they want a contemporary or a traditional design, wood is the *non plus ultra*. A material of immense versatility for both cabinets and work surfaces, one that seems almost to live and breathe, wood is so versatile – so many things to all men. The variety of timber types available is vast, and having more

THIS PAGE Wood works every time: simple, rough-planked cupboard doors with traditional country hinges and pull handles on the drawers are pleasingly combined with a traditional ceramic Belfast sink.

or less shaken off its scrubbed pine image (although that can still be a good look, if it is used with restraint and without the addition of dried, dusty flower swags), the decorative possibilities of wood are endless. Whether you choose solid wood or a wood veneer, you can find a natural finish in a wide range of shades and tones, which can be waxed and polished or sealed; or alternatively, look for a wood base that can be painted and generally decorated in any number of styles. Properly prepared, wood is hardwearing, extremely low maintenance and looks better and better over the years. Although many kitchens combine different types and colours of wood in work surfaces and cabinets, wood also takes very kindly to being paired with other materials as diverse as granite, stainless steel, Corian and

ABOVE LEFT Fitted, painted wooden units are combined with an unfitted, well-worn and much-used butcher's block on top of open shelves. Fruit and vegetables are tucked away in wicker baskets.

ABOVE RIGHT A kitchen that uses wood in many different guises – from the sealed, polished wooden floor to the painted and distressed table and chairs, as well as the decorative antique clock.

marble, where the contrast gives an added textural and visual interest to the whole.

As always, colour is an important element of any room, and the colours you use have a distinct bearing on how comfortable you feel in any room – in the kitchen particularly, perhaps because of all the functional equipment that is required. It's interesting that although colour in the kitchen is so important, many people prefer to keep the background fairly neutral and introduce colour through other elements – this might be with foodstuffs, plants and herbs, or linen, china and glass. If, however, you prefer to have some colour on the walls, keeping within the culinary comfort zone would seem to suggest colours that are warm but also fresh – soft yellows, browny-pinks, shades of turquoise and spring greens.

LEFT Wicker baskets, always a practical storage solution, have been used here in a semi-decorative way, housed in open unit shelving, either on their own or combined with other pieces of equipment.

RIGHT This large kitchen combines fitted work and storage units at one end, with an island unit and stools in the centre of the room. A long, family wooden dining table takes up the rest of the space.

A comfortable kitchen is almost always decorative; not because of all the fancy paint effects but because of all the interesting and attractive things on view; some that have a practical function, others that are displayed purely for their charm. Really comfortable kitchens, even if they have been decorated professionally, tend not to look as if they have been thought about a great deal; instead, they often give the impression that their owner has left out pieces – functional, practical and decorative – that he or she really likes and takes pleasure in having around. It might be china and glass – favourite shapes and quirky pieces – or it might be semi-useful objects – from mixing bowls to storage jars, wooden spoons and old weighing machines. And again, it might be books – cookery books and others besides – as well as pictures, flowers and plants, fresh fruit and vegetables. The table will be laid with care – a tablecloth is a very cozy thing to see on a table, (as long as it is clean; dirty, stained cloths have no place in the comfortable kitchen), as are cheerful napkins. And when the table has been set with china and glass that have been chosen for how they look as well as for how well they do the job, your cozy kitchen is complete.

THIS PAGE What could be simpler than an easy solution for tidy storage in this all-white kitchen? A piece of hemmed white fabric, tied with contrasting ribbon, is strung along a painted metal bar.

Last but very far from least, remember that however much effort and thought you put into how the kitchen looks, a truly comfortable kitchen is one in which it is immediately evident that someone actually cooks there. For some people, the idea of cooking as an intrinsic part of domestic life seems fraught with peril, but you don't have to be Gordon Ramsay to cook well. You do need to know the difference between a good ingredient and a bad one, and you do need to conquer any fear of cooking and learn one or two simple combinations that will always work and give pleasure and satisfaction, not only to those who eat with you but also to yourself. The thing about cooking is that the more you practise a dish, the better you become at it, so the ultimate culinary trick is to perfect a couple of really easy dishes. Who, after all, isn't capable of putting

some sprigs of tarragon and a lump of butter inside a chicken and roasting it in a hot oven for an hour? Or of sweating an onion and some garlic in olive oil before adding fresh or canned tomatoes and simmering for half an hour, to produce a rich tomato sauce to serve on spaghetti with some grated Parmesan on top? This is comfort food in its truest form – not complicated restaurant dishes with juliennes of this and reductions of that, but food that is simple and fresh, made with good quality ingredients; food that appeals on every level to those who eat it.

BELOW LEFT Textiles always work well in the cozy kitchen, adding an element of warmth. Here, fabric has been loosely gathered behind glass cupboard doors, and used to make full curtains around the open shelves.

BELOW RIGHT A kitchen where family life is in evidence; from the parked scooter to the artwork and abundance of plants.

RIGHT Dog décor at its most comfortable.

FAR RIGHT The most basic of coffee tables – the proverbial orange box even – is transformed into a pleasing and elegant piece of furniture with the help of a tailored white cloth.

BELOW Kindling and logs stored in a woven cane basket look immediately welcoming, with the promise of long evenings around warm fires.

the comfortable living room

The living room is, by its very nature, indelibly associated with the idea of comfort – it is the pleasurable part of the house where the family comes to relax and sit at ease.

An uncomfortable living room would be more than a contradiction in terms; it would also be a very unpleasant place indeed in which to spend time. The problem though is that, for some, the concept of comfort does not seem to be compatible with the idea of a well-decorated room. For these doubters who are suspicious of the very idea of 'decoration', a comfortable room is one where, vaguely, anything goes, where dogs lie sprawled on blanket-covered sofas (undeniably, that is comfortable, should you happen to be a dog), where dented cushions rest against the legs of chairs, where newspapers are spread over every surface and coffee mugs jostle for places on the floor and tables. In contrast, to these sceptics, a 'decorated' living room means a room of pristine regularity, of a particular fastidiousness; all plumped white cushions and feet-off chairs. So to write about decorating ideas for the comfortable living room can all too easily seem like a contradiction in terms.

THIS PAGE Comfort doesn't mean over-stuffed or overdone. Although this sitting room is furnished simply, every element, from the rug to the welcoming sofa cushions, makes this a room in which to while away idle time.

But, in fact, the two are not mutually exclusive; there is no reason why comfort may not be brought into the decorating equation. Who has not inwardly groaned on entering yet another cold, impersonal room, a room concerned solely with its visual impact and designed to be looked at rather than lived in. Good decoration is not shallow but personal, and is all to do with comfort; it is, however, the comfort of others, rather than one's own, that is the key to success – the art of making others feel at home.

One of the most important elements in the truly comfortable room is physical warmth, which in most people's minds equates with mental warmth. An open fire is of course not necessary – although extremely nice if you are in a position to have one – but an all-round pleasant temperature certainly is important, coupled with an absence of chilly draughts sliding in through windows and doors. Employ draught excluders, curtains and shutters – whatever you need to make the room a pleasure to be in.

Once the heating is sorted out, the next aspect to look at is the seating: comfortable decorating is about the feeling of contentment and ease that it engenders, and also about the physical sensations experienced. Although it may seem obvious, chairs and sofas should be a pleasure to sit on. This is not

ABOVE Washable loose covers on chairs and sofas are an instantaneous comfort factor. Their soft lines and slightly rumpled appearance suggest cozy afternoons curled up reading and talking.

FAR LEFT A foot stool of the same height and of equal dimensions to an armchair is an extremely useful piece of furniture. It can be used either to turn the chair into an instant daybed, coupled with a soft blanket, or as an extra, flexible seat.

ABOVE Whatever else a living room lacks, a deep-seated armchair, preferably with feather-stuffed cushions, in which you can relax with a book is a comfort essential.

ABOVE RIGHT Surfaces are important: for well-placed and convenient lighting, obviously, but also as somewhere for flowers, ornaments and a library resting place.

FAR RIGHT Comfort is not only found in conventional chairs and sofas. Here, an antique iron bed with cushions stacked against the foot and headboard is as cozy a spot as can be.

always a given, and indeed has not always even been seen as a necessity.

Although by the 5th century BC the Ancient Greeks had just about perfected chair design, epitomized by the elegant concave-backed, curved-leg chair known as the klismos and depicted on numerous stele and carvings of the period, somehow in Europe in the intervening centuries the art of comfortable chair design was lost. In the Middle Ages, for example, amongst other things, people wanted their houses to be warm with huge fireplaces in the communal hall and tapestries to fend off the cold weather on the walls. They wanted to parade their status to the outside world – as in cupboards set with the family plate, richly ornamented bed hangings and personal dress. The one thing that they did not seem to particularly desire was comfort – think of those primitive, straight-backed and hard wooden chairs and beds, made and used for hundreds of years. Indeed, comfort in seating was not rediscovered until the 17th century when in

France furniture makers – *les ébénistes* – first began to make seating that suited the increasingly luxurious rooms of the period. Chairs were designed with the body of the sitter in mind and with fitted cushions that were shaped, padded and upholstered – in fact, actually designed to be comfortable.

And although the road to comfort has sometimes been a little lumpy and hard since then, today comfortable seating is within the grasp of everybody.

If you are looking for comfortable new chairs or sofas, it is perhaps a truism that you should go for pieces that are well

THIS PAGE Comfort resides in the details: flowers on the table, an upholstered armchair, well-placed reading lights and an open fire.

RIGHT Comfort, by its very nature, is informal, but even so there should still remain some element of structure; here, flexible seating works with stacking side tables to make an infinite variety of cozy options.

made – which usually means a solid wooden base, with robust springs that are handtied, and different layers of filling from burlap to feather pads covering the construction. The cushions might be made of a mixture of foam and fibre or, if you are a traditionalist, with feathers – a well-plumped, feather seat cushion is a very comfortable sight indeed. As far as style is concerned, the once popular three-piece sofa and chair suite is thankfully no longer considered the bee's knees – instead, a combination of shapes and sizes is a lot more flexible and suits many more people.

As far as the shape is concerned, a comfortable chair will obviously have been designed to support the body of the sitter – from legs to head and neck. Although there are now many, many designs available, both traditional and contemporary, the choice of a relatively classic style will mean that it can be reinvented and renewed over the years with changes of cover, both loose and upholstered.

The texture of the covering fabric should also be considered where comfort is a consideration: wool, tweed or even a kelim-type fabric can be uncomfortable and rough to sit on. Cotton, linen and linen mixes, however, are soft and inviting. Consider the pattern also – too strong a design with too many colours can be very limiting and quickly become

boring. A better idea might be to have a design that is in either one or two colours, or a self-pattern or weave. Apart from being easier to work into the rest of the room scheme, simple designs are better as a foil for our favourite room brightener and comfort magnet – the cushion!

Yes, square or rectangular, sausage-shaped or circular, trimmed and tasselled, and single or in pairs, every comfort zone requires cushions in a combination of colours and patterns to lean against, move around and just generally enjoy.

The comfortable living room must have enough places to put things on; ample small, relatively portable tables and surfaces in easy reach of chairs and sofas ready for the inevitable books, drinks and spectacles.

And although they are certainly not a necessity, it is true that most comfortable living rooms, whether they are close carpeted or have a tiled or wooden floor, are made even more comfortable with the addition of one or more rugs, which define areas within a room and give a focal point, and are also very nice for just sitting on in comfort. Obviously, the design or pattern of any rugs must not only work with each other, but also with other surface patterns and colour within the room. Remember to consider scale before choosing a particular rug – too small and the rest of the room appears unconnected; too large and everything within the room will seem cramped.

ABOVE LEFT The high-sided sofa is the most adaptable of designs, in that it can be used for sleeping as well as sitting!

LEFT Even a less-comfy sofa (not that this is) can be made inviting by adding cushions, cushions and more cushions.

THIS PAGE Different seating designs and shapes allow everyone to be easily accommodated on a variety of perches. A wide, low table, such as the one pictured, brings together the disparate sofa shapes.

Of course, to enjoy all these pleasurable activities there must also be lighting that highlights the different, carefully selected elements. Lighting in a sitting room should be infinitely adaptable, and the best lighting schemes involve a combination of various lighting types: first there is background or ambient lighting – perhaps a mixture of up- and downlighters and recessed lighting. Couple this with accent lighting – lighting that is used to bring interest and drama into a room, to highlight particular aspects of the room with a beam or pool of light onto a decorative object or into a specific part of the room, or simply some lights that are objects of interest and beauty in their own right. And finally, and very importantly from the comfort aspect of a room, there is what is rather baldly called task lighting – specific lights, thoughtfully placed, that allow you to read, draw, sew or chat

as you will. These may be table lamps of different heights and shapes and/or perhaps floor lamps with adjustable arms and shades. It is the mixture that is important; the variety that gives interest to a room – that – coupled with the lighting expert's eternal best friend, the dimmer button.

ABOVE LEFT A classic of its kind, the high-backed wing chair became popular in the 18th century as a gentleman's library chair, where he could sit in peace, protected from, but warmed by, the nearby open fire.

ABOVE RIGHT A sofa large enough to double as an occasional bed has an assortment of cushions and deep, feather seating, both of which invite extended stays.

LEFT Cushion covers do not have to be identical, nor do the shapes need to be uniform, but there must be a unifying strand – either of colour or design.

THIS PAGE If a sofa is comfortable enough – as this one is – to invite lengthy periods of relaxed reading, ensure that there are flexible lighting options to suit everybody's taste.

THIS PAGE Comfort is as much about arrangement as anything else – here it is expressed as having a bathroom close to hand, a large reading lamp and a pile of books ready to dip into. Time to go to bed!

the peaceful bedroom

For most people, the idea of a peaceful bedroom is usually synonymous with comfort, quiet and calm. Happily, though, such ideals are not actually difficult to achieve.

In any bedroom, the most important piece of furniture is the bed, for that is where comfort and peace begin. If the bed itself is uncomfortable, you will not sleep well, and if you do not sleep well, daily life becomes more and more trying until you find yourself in a tired cycle from which it can be hard to escape.

Today, mail order bedding companies and specialist shops cater to the widespread and natural desire for comfort; their brochures loaded with illustrations of every possible luxurious accoutrement – from linen sheets and cashmere blankets to down pillows and silk-filled duvets –

ABOVE LEFT The senses respond to a bedroom that is decorated appealingly. An old-fashioned white-painted wooden bed, pretty linen, a decorative blind and flowers in glass bottles have the effect of charming and welcoming the visitor.

ABOVE RIGHT Layers of warmth give a sense of reassuring comfort. A thick rug at the bottom of the bed and cushions covered with fringed blanketing look extremely cozy.

LEFT A sense of order is essential in a peaceful bedroom, exemplified by this set of baskets in which clothes can be stored.

all described in the same breathless manner as a menu in a three-star restaurant, and usually just as tempting.

But luxury is not always synonymous with comfort, and where the bed is concerned, comfort actually begins and ends with the mattress rather than the bed base. For, unless you are still in possession of a post-war utility bed with a sagging wire base that looks like an old string bag, the base of your bed will probably either be sprung, slatted or a platform, all of which can have long, useful lives and do not necessarily need to be replaced just because you need a new mattress.

If your mattress sinks or dips alarmingly, or you ache every morning, then it is time to replace it. Today's mattresses are obviously very different from the first simple mattress bags used thousands of years ago, which were stuffed with fillings of varying degrees of comfort depending on your status, wealth and the culture you lived in. Straw, reeds and hay for some; straw cotton, wool and horsehair for others. By the mid-18th century the mattress bag had evolved into a case that in turn, by the 19th century, became a spring-filled construction around which wool, cotton and other fibres were wrapped.

THIS PAGE An antique iron bed has been brought smartly up to date with crisp bed linen in a contemporary design, a folding butler's tray and a decorative set of graphic, monochrome prints.

THIS PAGE In an all-white room, an old wooden-sided bed that has been painted white is made up with fat pillows, spotty sheets and the simplest of flowery blinds, raised and lowered with the aid of ribbons.

BELOW A bed packed with pattern; an iron bedstead is covered with a bright antique patchwork quilt, the colours of which are emphasized by a group of colourful cushions.

To make the mattress more comfortable, on top of this firm base was usually added one, or sometimes several, smaller mattresses or feather beds – actually, more like a fat quilt than a mattress, and filled with either pure down or a feather and down mixture. Feather beds were in continual use until the 20th century – in 1847 Heal's, the famous London bed shop, was advertising a number of different down fillings to be purchased by the pound for DIY use, from Grey Goose at 1/4d (equivalent to 16 pence or around 25 cents) a lb, to 3/– (equivalent to 36 pence or around 60 cents) for the Best Danzig White Goose. Feather beds like these, portable and valuable (they were routinely willed to descendants), were accumulated. The wealthier you were, the more you might have layered on top of the basic mattress: the spoiled princess in Hans Christian Andersen's fairy story lay on top of 20 feather beds (and still she felt the peas).

The good news for comfort lovers is that you can still buy feather beds – or mattress comforters or toppers, as they are now often known (not to be confused with the more utilitarian mattress protectors). Designed to lie on top of an existing mattress, mattress comforters come in different styles and weights that range from a quilted fibre overlay (avoid the very thin ones) to styles made

ABOVE LEFT if you are lucky enough to have a bedroom with a deep windowsill, fill it with books, objects and above all fresh flowers from the garden.

RIGHT AND FAR RIGHT
This bedroom has been designed with total comfort in mind: a padded headboard, pillows and a well-upholstered daybed – in various designs and colourways of traditional 18th-century toile de Jouy. The antique armoire is a capacious, beautiful way of storing necessities.

BELOW Bright crocheted bed covers are seldom seen, which is a pity, since they are pretty and cozy.

from lambswool, natural latex and luxurious double-layered designs, the bottom layer consisting of stitched channelled feathers; the upper, boxed down. They are incredibly comfortable and add a whole new dimension of sink-in luxury to the bed.

The poor pillow is the Cinderella of the comfortable bed. While thought and money are spent on bed linen and covers, the pillow lies, for most of its unassuming life, unnoticed and without being remarked upon. If you can't remember when you last bought a new pillow or if you fold your pillow over your arm and it

doesn't immediately straighten up, then you know it's time to get a new one. Pillows come in different sizes and fillings. Buy the type and the shape that is most comfortable for you, rather than the cheapest.

What you lie on and under comes next, and bed linen is a topic on which everyone has an opinion (although most will agree that all natural fibres are better than synthetic weaves, which don't breathe, can pill and bobble, and snag your toenails to boot). It really is impossible to categorically say that linen or silk is better than cotton, as what you sleep in is always a very personal choice. If, for example, you like a very soft sheet, then Percale cotton with a very high thread count (the number of threads in a square inch) might be your choice; if a smooth finish seems very inviting, the gleam of a cotton sateen sheet can do the trick; and if you prefer the cool but slightly coarser feel of pure linen, then nothing else will do.

Try not to economize too much on sheets. All linen companies have good half-yearly sales, and bed linen – if it is plain coloured, and particularly if it is plain white – hardly goes out of fashion. Moreover, the designs can be intermixed. It is fun, and indeed satisfying, to add to your linen cupboard in the manner of a trousseau collector of old, with one or two carefully chosen additions every year.

Lighting is the next, and very important, comfort element in a bedroom – both lighting that you want and, just as important, the lighting – or light – that you don't want. It is a fact that we all sleep better in a dark (and relatively cool) room, so the windows should be made as lightproof as possible. If your preference is for roller blinds, consider installing a coated blackout blind, set flush to the window frame. These blinds, which when properly installed can completely block out the light, are no longer simply black – they come in every colour imaginable as well as in many patterned designs, and they can be used in conjunction with a Roman blind. They also work well beneath curtains – which should be at the very least lined, and perhaps interlined too.

The lighting that you do want – in the form of electric lamps and background lighting – should ideally be on dimmer switches for really flexible comfort. If, rather than swing-arm wall lights, you prefer bedside reading lights, do make sure that these are tall enough (and bright enough) to throw a beam of light down onto a book if you are sitting up in bed. Peering at a book sideways beneath a toadstool bedside light is the very opposite of comfort and will strain your eyes too.

Finally colour – perhaps the most undervalued,

FAR LEFT A light hand with the decorative touches is best in the bedroom. Here, a quilt-bedecked bed is bordered by antique dressmakers' frames to hold costume jewellery.

ABOVE There is something intrinsically romantic about a bed hung with simple curtains, even though as in the case of this gauzy mosquito net, they also have a practical purpose.

yet important aspect of a comfortable, peaceful room. In the bedroom, it is always better to choose colours that are calm in tone, rather than overstimulating. However, instead of just plumping for wall-to-wall magnolia, look at some paint shade cards; there are probably hundreds of different variations of neutral colours, from white and off-whites, to ivories, creams and stone. Think of them as tones to use together, perhaps with another complementary colour, and a harmonious, subtle scheme will be the result.

the practical bathroom

The ritual of washing has not always been the most popular of pastimes. Throughout the ages societies have fallen in and out of love with the idea of sweet-smelling cleanliness.

BELOW The simplest of bathrooms can still give practical pleasure and comfort; a clean bathroom with scented soap and a wooden towel horse with fresh, white towels to hand are all that is needed.

BELOW RIGHT Bathroom storage is key to comfort: open wooden shelving is cheap to buy and easy to install, and can hold all necessities, from towels to toothbrushes.

The Ancient Romans' love of bathing, both in private and public baths, is well documented and witnessed, and more than a thousand years later numerous medieval illustrations attest to bathing as a jolly, social and sometimes erotic activity with wooden tubs for two often depicted.

In the 16th and 17th centuries, however, citizens did not seem to be overly concerned about bathing in particular, or indeed about personal cleanliness in general. Though at Versailles – where so many innovations in interior decoration and design were initiated –

bathrooms for the royal family were installed, but not public privies (commentators of the time remarked on the smell in the palace corridors, which were used as handy, if smelly, urinals by courtiers and visitors). Even when bathrooms began very slowly to be installed across Europe, most rich people still bathed in a tub in front of the fire, filled with endless buckets of hot water brought to the tub by someone else. Indeed, in 19th-century England there were still few bathrooms, and those that were installed were far from comfortable places – a trend that continued

THIS PAGE Wood and glass, white on white, nothing excessive, nothing unnecessary – this bathroom is a fine example of how to create style without expense.

THIS PAGE As compact as in a ship's cabin, this cleverly designed bathroom combines practicality with decorative flourish, exemplified by the teardrop chandelier and massive storage chest.

for at least another hundred years. You don't have to be that old to remember grim, unheated bathrooms where taking a bath was a test of endurance involving sub-zero air temperatures, cold floors, thin towels and lukewarm water.

But that was then. Today, all is very different – designers have moved on from the kitchen into the bathroom; indeed, for some, the bathroom is the new kitchen. The once functional room has been transformed: spa baths with whirlpool systems and sequential underwater mood lighting; showers that become mini steam rooms or that are equipped with powerful massage jets. The bathroom has changed from a place of uncomfortable if necessary ablutions to a pleasure palace. In estate agents' particulars, every noteworthy feature is described, in glowing, fully illustrated detail.

But is such overt luxury and innovation quite the same as being comfortable? I don't think so, for the fact is that a truly comfortable bathroom in which one wants to linger and leaves refreshed can actually be achieved without too many, if any, state of the art devices.

The first thing to consider is that most essential element: warmth. If neither you nor the bathroom is warm, you can never be comfortable, so ensure that the room is free of draughts and install a radiator or, even better, a heated towel rail – the largest size you can fit against the wall, and filled with oversized, fluffy towels. Towels should be renewed when they lose their fluffiness – they don't dry you as quickly, and so the all-important, comfort-making element is lost.

For many, bathroom comfort can be epitomized by a deep, warm bath, and today it is not always

ABOVE This is a bathroom to linger in with its large mirror, carefully hung pictures and a pile of books waiting on a handy stool.

LEFT In a small bathroom, a clever integral storage unit combines cupboards for things best kept out of sight with cut-out niches for the more decorative aspects of bathroom life.

LEFT A free-standing sink unit has been made from a simple wooden table. Bathroom paraphernalia looks far better stored in wicker baskets than left on view.

ABOVE A chair is always a welcome addition to a bathroom, to sit on and chat or even to store towels on. Although space saving, wall hooks are all the more practical.

necessary to automatically throw out the well-shaped but tired old bath for the spanking new; technological advances mean that an old bath, whether it is metal, ceramic or even plastic, cannot only be resurfaced but chips mended or even the existing colour altered.

A comfortable bathroom is one where all the necessary accessories, from bottles and jars to bath and shower, have a place – preferably out of sight, so as much storage as possible is vital. Not always considered in the original plan, you can, in fact, never have too much storage space in a bathroom. A cupboard beneath the basin is a good, if obvious, idea, but also if your bath is enclosed by fixed panels, consider the wasted

storage space around the base of the bath therein; make use of it by having a section of the panel set with hidden hinges and an invisible push-to-open mechanism. A bathroom mirrored cabinet, particularly one with integral lighting, is also useful.

There is quite often extra, unused wall space in a bathroom. Put in some shelves – glass ones are a good way of maximizing space – or even a small cupboard. And don't forget some storage for books near the toilet – a shelf, stool or a basket.

Good and adaptable lighting is an important part of the comfortable bathroom. Lighting regulations are pretty rigorous for obvious safety reasons, so whatever lighting choices you make – carefully positioned downlighters perhaps,

THIS PAGE All the frills of the fair are here in this otherwise simply decorated bathroom: a bath-shaped oval rail, attached from the ceiling, supports striped, frilled curtains – glamorous enough for a party.

THIS PAGE Comfortable bathrooms do not always have to be all new and all modern. Here, an old, free-standing bath is installed in a room painted in soft blue-greys and whites to create a wonderfully harmonious space.

with task lighting over and around the basin – have dimmer switches installed outside the door to regulate the lighting within. And good scented candles are always a bathroom lighting bonus.

There is no regulation that says you may not hang pictures in a bathroom. The space, as long as it does not get too steamed up, is often an ideal size to hang smaller pictures and photographs that might be lost elsewhere. Plus there is the added bonus of being able to contemplate them in aqueous comfort.

And finally, remember that good soap – perhaps the ultimate bathing luxury – is a very good investment for a very small outlay.

ABOVE LEFT Try to look for pretty containers for bathroom bits; glass jars are good, but so are odd, pretty pieces of china such as spare cups and saucers rescued from the back of the cupboard.

ABOVE CENTRE Rather than keeping toilet paper in sight, store it in a basket.

ABOVE RIGHT Instead of conventional soap dishes, old terracotta plates can be put to decorative use.

BELOW Comfort is a long soak in a warm bath with a soothing hot drink and scented candles for company. Instead of a traditional metal rack, a made-to-size wooden board fits the bill perfectly.

ABOVE Whatever their original intention, pretty pots, mugs and glasses will always make original and charming pen and pencil holders.

the satisfying study

The frenetic pace of life in the 21st century means that we all need somewhere at home, even if it is just a flat surface in a corner, from which we can work, whether it is keeping track of bills and correspondence or writing that next great novel.

But that doesn't mean to say such a space has to be utilitarian and cold, or to remind you – as the term 'home office' can so often do – of grey filing cabinets and dusty Swiss cheese plants. So rather than thinking 'office', instead turn your mind to the idea of a study. It is an evocative, romantic word that brings to mind a comfortable, quiet room, warm and well lit, with deep armchairs, a pretty desk and walls lined with interesting

books and pictures. Although for most of us the realization of such a luxurious room, large and wholly dedicated to our pursuits alone, is but an ideal, there is no reason, even if you can only muster half a wall in a room that also serves another purpose, why the idea of a comfortable, satisfying study should not be yours.

Obviously, the first task is to identify where it could be, and although there may not be a large

ABOVE Use your study for all manner of occupations such as old-fashioned crafting. Pleasurable sewing requires everything to be close to hand, as well as very good natural light.

FAR LEFT A satisfying study does not have be equipped with conventional office furniture. Instead of a desk, a long trestle table and a pair of workmanlike chairs are all that is required.

FAR RIGHT A satisfying
study is one where all
needs are easily, simply
to hand: a wooden table,
adjustable light, large
waste paper basket and
a wall of books. Sorted!

BELOW The smallest corner
can be made individual as
long as it is marked out as
a personal space, as has
been done here with some
books and pictures.

room available, there may be somewhere smaller – a single bedroom perhaps, or even somewhere almost too small for much else other than storage that could be commandeered. Or look at dead, dark spaces not normally considered as rooms – off the kitchen, beneath a well-proportioned staircase or on a landing; clever, contemporary lighting, coupled with intelligent shelving, can brilliantly transform areas like these. But if all these options fail, last but actually by no means least is a workspace in part of a larger room –

kitchen, living room or bedroom, either open or closed; perhaps inside a cupboard that opens to reveal desk space, shelves and essential equipment.

Wherever it is positioned, the key is to make this workspace seem a satisfying study and, as so often in the comfortable home, this starts with the concept of order – essential where pieces of paper and folders are concerned – so well-thought-out storage is the key, with everything that you need in its place and easily to hand, although not necessarily on view.

Containers for files and papers range from the resoundingly functional filing cabinets – thankfully, no longer just grey or black but available in slightly more cheerful colours and finishes; you can of course always change the colour of a metal cabinet yourself with a bit of prepping and judicious use of a spray paint. Then there is the more subtle approach, perhaps more suited to a home office, using storage that ranges from purpose-designed rattan and wicker paper trays, storage baskets and file containers, to wooden and cardboard boxes in every pattern, size and colour. And for those who prefer to use what they already have to hand, baskets of every shape and size will always work well, particularly as containers for different-coloured plastic files.

If your study is set up against a wall, the 'desk' can of course be any flat surface – which actually often looks much better in a domestic setting than would a conventional, and much more expensive, office piece. Options include an old wooden table that may have been painted to fit in with the room, a cheap and cheerful trestle or a piece of wood or MDF/particleboard cut to fit and set below shelves of a similar material.

Shelves – or at least a shelf – are, I think, key to the idea of a satisfying study. On a shelf, not only can you keep any files and ledgers but also box files, books and anything else you might want to refer to or that you just like to look at. Open shelves are the ultimate simple storage system – easy to see and also easy to access.

It really is important to try and get a good, comfortable chair if you are going to spend any amount of time at your desk. A purpose-designed office chair is not of course compulsory, but do at least look for a chair that gives the right support for your spine. Also, a chair with elbow supports will help to avoid strain on your neck.

Make sure that the area is well lit – for although daylight is good, for real comfort, you will definitely also need some dedicated, focused task lighting, such as an anglepoise/gooseneck lamp with a directional beam or a table lamp that throws light over your work.

Finally, get personal – have flowers on your desk; add pictures, objects and photographs that mean something to you and that give you pleasure. And don't be afraid to update or rotate these personal touches once in a while. It is these seemingly small details that make this workspace a study; not an office. And in the comfortable home, that is a very good thing.

LEFT A study does not have to be a book room; everyone needs a place where they can keep their personal belongings and deal with daily life.

RIGHT The smaller the space, the more important it is to customize it: a wall covered with personal mementoes, pictures and memorabilia quickly does the trick.

conservatories and garden rooms

If comfort is about making your guests feel welcome, there can be few more comfort-enducing signs than a serried line of gum boots standing near a garden door, or another open door leading into a welcoming conservatory, with the garden beyond. Both speak volumes not only of the possibilities thereof but also of your wish to allow your guests to immerse themselves in the joys of the garden, both indoors and out.

The greater and smaller pleasures of the garden, including the collection and cultivation of plants, have always been important. By the 17th century, in the grounds of larger houses, orangeries – large masonry structures with wide glazed areas – were often constructed for the overwintering of the newly fashionable citrus trees as well as other tender exotic plants.

Two centuries on, new manufacturing and construction methods, coupled with new developments in metalworking, meant that metal and glass could be relatively easily combined to build a conservatory – a light and airy interpretation of the orangery, and one that became hugely popular. Blame it all on Joseph Paxton and the success of the enormous glasshouse that he designed and built for the sixth Duke of Devonshire at Chatsworth, which covered three-quarters of an acre (3,000 square metres). It was enlivened by tropical birds and pools filled with goldfish and was bisected by a central carriageway, which was lit by 12,000 lamps when Queen Victoria drove through it on a visit in 1843. Paxton was commissioned to design the Crystal Palace in Hyde Park for the

LEFT Many conservatories were originally designed to be greenhouses where seedlings and plants could be cultivated; such a space is a recipe for relaxation and satisfaction.

RIGHT This conservatory is an ideal extra living space. The painted brick walls, retractable blind and polished wooden floor, along with personal touches, make it perfect.

THIS PAGE A light and airy garden room or conservatory is often used as an additional eating space – right for every meal, from a sunny breakfast to a candlelit dinner.

Great Exhibition of 1851 – a towering edifice that rose 108 feet (33 metres) into the sky and covered 19 acres (77 square metres) of the Park's expanse.

The conservatories that were then added in numbers to houses old and new were sometimes used as a decorative and practical link to the garden or for the cultivation of delicate pot plants and flowers for the house. Larger edifices were also used to grow exotic fruits normally found in sunnier climes for the dinner table. The Rothschild family's conservatories at their various mansions were particularly famed for their cultivation of such delicacies – Meyer de Rothschild even had a grove of banana trees in his glasshouse at Mentmore.

Conservatories were also designed to become what was almost an extra reception room; a winter garden where less formal, more intimate

life could be pursued. Some were wildly romantic and Russian winter gardens were especially famed. Drawings and paintings show them flanked with exotic flowering shrubs and trees such as magnolia and camellia, orchids, roses and jasmine – the air must have been impregnated with their rich scent.

But what goes up, certainly in conservatory terms, must usually come down; and these hard-to-heat structures fell out of favour and into disrepair by the middle of the 20th century, only

ABOVE This conservatory succeeds perfectly in bringing the garden into the house, acting as a wonderfully verdant link between inside and out.

LEFT An easy-to-carry chair set up in a sunny corner of a small conservatory makes the perfect spot for some warm rest and relaxation.

LEFT The simplest of indoor/outdoor spaces can be made congenial with the addition of garden chairs and a wooden table.

RIGHT An old-fashioned conservatory was always about creating the perfect combination of plant house and living space; here, vines and other climbers share the space with comfy chairs and a table.

BELOW Terracotta, metal, even plastic; plants and seedlings can be grown and nurtured in any container that comes to hand. Clumped together, they are always pleasing in a garden room.

to rise again, phoenix-like, in the 1970s and '80s when further advances in design meant that new conservatories could be easily constructed and attached to an existing building, providing what was in effect a now easily heated extra room for a relatively modest outlay.

Modern conservatories do not, on the whole, take well to being furnished with the same sort of overstuffed, upholstered furniture seen in 19th-century paintings and photographs. Comfortable informality is the key and as such is far more easily achieved with wicker chairs filled with fat cushions on which to lounge on an inclement day, or to sit amongst the roses with

LEFT Happy is the owner of a traditional porch: for hundreds of years this coveted space outside the house has been perfect for talking, relaxing or just watching the world go by.

BELOW A terrace is a continuation of the house inside and should be treated as such with comfortable chairs and tables. Plants and shrubs give additional pleasure.

RIGHT Add lighting to a garden space: tea lights and candles can be set up on tables, on the ground and in holders planted in the soil or hung from sturdy branches.

a glass of wine in the early evening. And should there be the floor space, a rug or mat (think kelim or sisal) adds warmth to the area. If the conservatory is to be used as an extra (or indeed sole) eating space, again think simple – a traditional dining suite simply does not look right – better by far that there be almost a picnic atmosphere about the arrangement. A trestle table with

cotton cloth and fold-up wooden chairs gives the right air of *déjeuner* almost *sur l'herbe,* and encourages diners to feel at ease. Add a few terracotta pots of ever-forgiving geraniums and herbs – the scent of verbena is particularly delicious – and the scene is set.

A conservatory is of course not the only way of enjoying garden life from a safe distance. There is the garden room, which might be an appendage to the house – a glorified potting shed, if truth be told, or even a separate structure, installed in the garden itself, where work can be done, tea can be taken and novels read. It can even be a terrace or a porch adjoining the house.

The point is that regardless of whether you opt for a conservatory, garden room or simply being outdoors, make it enticing, with cushions at the very least, a bench, chairs – after all, it's a place to relax and reflect on the true comforts of life.

index

Page numbers in *italic* refer
to the illustrations

UK & US sources

GENERAL

Habitat
www.habitat.co.uk
Stylish, contemporary homewares.

The House Directory
www.thehousedirectory.com
*An online directory of unusual
and interesting homeware shops.*

IKEA
www.ikea.com
*Fabulous for well-priced home
and outdoor products.*

John Lewis
+44 (0)3456 049049
www.johnlewis.co.uk
*Department stores with
everything for the home.*

Laura Ashley
www.lauraashley.com
www.lauraashleyusa.com
*English-garden-look floral, striped,
checked and solid cotton fabrics
for every room in the house.*

ABC Carpet & Home
www.abchome.com
*Home furnishing, fabrics, carpets
and accessories.*

Anthropologie
www.anthropologie.com
*One-of-a-kind home accessories.
Available to buy online.*

Barneys at Saks
www.saksfifthavenue.com
*Home furnishings and
accessories.*

Bloomingdale's
www.bloomingdales.com
*Department store with many
locations across the US.*

CB2
www.cb2.com
*Affordable, modern homewares
for every room of the house.*

Crate & Barrel
www.crateandbarrel.com
*Good-value furniture and
accessories.*

Lexington Home Brands
www.lexington.com
Wide range of home furnishings.

Pottery Barn
www.potterybarn.com
*Good for all homeware needs,
especially outdoor furnishings.*

Target
+1 800 440 0680
www.target.com
*Good value bedding, kitchenware,
bath accessories and furniture.*

FABRICS

Anta
+44 (0)1862 832477
www.anta.co.uk
*Plaids and checks in colours
inspired by Scotland.*

Bennison Fabrics
www.bennisonfabrics.com
*Tea-stained chintzes, florals,
stripes and damasks.*

Cabbages and Roses
www.cabbagesandroses.com
Faded florals by the metre.

Cath Kidston
www.cathkidston.com
*1950s-style florals, accessories
and fabrics.*

Chelsea Textiles
40–42 Pimlico Road
London SW1W 8LP
+44 (0)20 7584 5544
www.chelseatextiles.com
*Gorgeous embroidered cottons,
delicate prints, linens, silks and
voiles with an 18th-century feel.*

The Cloth Shop
290 Portobello Road
London W10 5TE
+44 (0)20 8968 6001
www.theclothshop.net
Well-priced natural fibres.

Designers Guild
www.designersguild.com
*Fresh, pretty designs for curtains
and upholstery.*

D. Porthault
470 Park Avenue
New York, NY 10022
+1 212 688 1660
www.dporthaultparis.com
*Beautiful printed and embroidered
bed linen and textiles.*

Ian Mankin
Studio 11, Worlds End Studios
Lots Road
London SW10 0RJ
+44 (0)20 7722 0997
www.ianmankin.co.uk
Canvas, ticking, cotton and linen.

Linen Me
23 Glendale Close
St Johns
Woking
Surrey GU21 3HN
+44 (0)20 8133 3853
www.linenme.com
*Linen fabrics, striped tablecloths
and more.*

MacCulloch & Wallis
25–26 Poland Street
London W1F 8QN
+44 (0)20 7629 0311
www.macculloch-wallis.co.uk
*Great range of fabrics and
trimmings.*

Calico
www.calicocorners.com
*Retailer of fabric designers such
as Justina Blakeley and Vern Yip.*

Garnet Hill
www.garnethill.com
*Bedding, linens and home
accessories.*

The Stripes Company
Unit 1, Waverton Business Park
Saighton Ln, Waverton
Chester CH3 7PD
+44 (0)1244 336 387
www.thestripescompany.com
*Striped deckchair fabrics and
home and garden accessories.*

Yves Delorme
www.yvesdelorme.com
Sophisticated linens.

FURNITURE

Bed Bazaar
The Old Station
Station Road
Framlingham
Suffolk IP13 9EE
+44 (0)1278 723756
www.bedbazaar.co.uk
Antique bedsteads.

The Old Cinema
160 Chiswick High Road
London W4 1PR
+44 (0)20 8995 4166
www.theoldcinema.co.uk
*Founded in 1978, this west
London antiques emporium is
home to thousands of pieces
across three storeys.*

The French Bed Company
PO Box 145
Newport
Essex CB11 3ZX
+44 (0)1799 542847
www.thefrenchbedcompany.co.uk
Beds with a romantic feel.

George Smith Sofas
www.georgesmith.com
Traditional upholstered furniture.

The Home Depot
www.homedepot.com
*Great furnishings and other
homewares.*

Ligne Roset
www.ligne-roset.com
Sleek, modern furniture and more.

OKA
+44 (0)3330 042042
www.oka.com
*Good quality furnishings in classic,
contemporary and traditional styles.*

Scumble Goosie
www.scumblegoosie.co.uk
*Vintage-inspired painted and
unpainted furniture.*

West Elm
www.westelm.com
*Contemporary furniture and
accessories.*

HOMEWARE

Atlantic Blankets
1 Westcott House, St Pirans Road
Perranporth
Cornwall TR6 0BH
+44 (0)1872 573259
www.atlanticblankets.com
Gorgeous blankets and throws.

Baileys Home Store
Whitecross Farm
Bridstow HR9 6JU
+44 (0)1989 561931
www.baileyshome.com
*Beautiful, simply designed
household objects.*

Labour and Wait
85 Redchurch Street
London E2 7DJ
+44 (0)20 7729 6253
www.labourandwait.co.uk
*Beautiful old-fashioned household
brushes and kitchen utensils.*

Ochre
+44 (0)20 7096 7372
+1 212 414 4332
www.ochre.net
*Contemporary yet timeless
furniture, lighting and accessories.*

Toast
www.toa.st
Beautiful items for the home.

The White Company
+44 (0)20 3758 9222
www.thewhitecompany.com
*Fine-quality bed linen, towels,
furnishings and accessories.*

KITCHENS & BATHROOMS

Antique Baths of Ivybridge
Erme Bridge Works
Ermington Road, Ivybridge
Devon PL21 9DE
+44 (0)1752 698250
www.antiquebaths.com
*Bathtub restoration, plus old
and repro tubs for sale.*

The Dormy House
27 Walworth Business Park
Andover
Hampshire SP10 5LH
+44 (0)1264 365808
www.thedormyhouse.com
*Cabinetry ranges that include
linen cupboards and larders.*

Plain English
28 Blandford Street
London W1U 4BZ
+44 (0)20 7486 2674
+1 212 203 0726
www.plainenglishdesign.co.uk
Handcrafted bespoke kitchens.

The Water Monopoly
10/14 Lonsdale Road
London NW6 6RD
+44 (0)20 7624 2636
www.thewatermonopoly.com
*Vintage-inspired and restored
antique sanitaryware.*

Bed Bath & Beyond
www.bedbathandbeyond.com
Everything for bed and bath.

P.E. Guerin
+1 212 243 5270
www.peguerin.com
Decorative hardware.

RH
+1 800 762 1005
www.rh.com
*Good for lighting, bed and bath
linens and more.*

LIGHTING

Graham and Green
92 Walcot Street
Bath BA1 5BG
+44 (0)1225 418200
www.grahamandgreen.co.uk
*Great for lighting as well as
glass, cushions and tableware.*

Hector Finch
90 Wandsworth Bridge Road
London SW6 2TF
+44 (0)20 7731 8886
www.hectorfinch.com
Antique and reproduction lighting.

London Lighting
+44 (0)20 3507 1911
www.londonlighting.co.uk
Designer lighting.

Top Brass Lighting
www.topbrasslighting.com
Unique lamps and lighting.

The Urban Electric Co.
2120 Noisette Boulevard
North Charleston, SC 29405
www.urbanelectric.com
*All kinds of beautiful lights, from
simple wall sconces to statement
pendants and chandeliers.*

PAINT

Farrow & Ball
+44 (0)1202 876141
www.farrow-ball.com (UK & US)
Heritage paint colours.

Milkpaint
1617 East Meadowbrook Drive
Tooele, Utah 84074
+1 435 255 4556
www.milkpaint.com
*Paints made from eco-friendly
natural pigments.*

Pratt and Lambert Paints
+1 800 289 7728
www.prattandlambert.com
*150-year-old producer of top
of the line paints.*

STORAGE

A Place for Everything
+44 (0)1244 680501
www.aplaceforeverything.co.uk
Storage with style.

Lakeland
+44 (0)1539 488100
www.lakeland.co.uk
*Great for all sorts of storage
solutions, including cheap
plastic storage boxes.*

Muji
www.muji.com
www.muji.us
*Fantastic and durable storage
at good prices.*

WALLPAPERS

Cole & Son
www.cole-and-son.com
Fine hand-printed wallpapers.

Colefax and Fowler
www.colefax.com
English wallpapers and fabrics.

EW Moore
41–43 Plashet Grove
London E6 1AD
+44 (0)20 8471 9392
www.ewmoore.com
A selection of vintage wallpapers.

Lewis & Wood
Woodchester Mill
North Woodchester
Stroud
Gloucestershire GL5 5NN
+44 (0)1453 878517
www.lewisandwood.co.uk
*Gloriously eccentric wallpapers
and fabrics.*

Thibaut
www.thibautdesign.com
Speciality wallpapers.

ANTIQUE MARKETS

Camden Passage
The Angel, Islington
London N1 8ED
*Open Wednesday through
Sunday every week.*

Portobello Road Market
Portobello Road
London W10 5TY
www.portobelloroad.co.uk
Open every Saturday.

Chelsea Flea
29 West 25th Street
New York, NY 10010
www.chelseaflea.com
Open every Saturday and Sunday.

Rose Bowl Flea Market
1001 Rose Bowl Drive
Pasadena, CA 91103
+1 323 560 7469
www.rgcshows.com
*Open the second Sunday of
every month.*

business credits

Architects, designers and businesses whose work and products are featured in this book.

A

Adamczewski
196 High Street
Lewes
East Sussex BN7 2NS
pages 19l

An Angel at my Table
www.anangelatmytable.com
pages 16r, 57c, 72-73, 117al

Andrew Treverton
+44 (0)7799 586810
pages 56, 62r, 112bl

Annabel Grey
+44 (0)7860 500356
annabel.grey@btinternet.com
www.annabelgrey.com
pages 25, 43r, 80

Arne Maynard
www.arne-maynard.com
page 144l

Arne Tengblad
Arteng@wanadoo.fr
+ 33 4 90 72 38 44
and Linum
+33 4 90 76 34 00
contact@linum-france.com
www.linum-france.com
page 27c

B

Baileys
Whitecross Farm
Bridstow
Herefordshire HR9 6JU
+44 (0)1989 561931
www.baileys-home-garden.co.uk
pages 54, 66ar, 98

Beach Studios
www.beachstudios.co.uk
+44 (0)1797 344077
pages 1, 3, 4, 9, 18, 23l, 27r, 30-31, 36–37, 55, 77c, 79, 81, 82al, 82b, 90–91, 112–113, 116, 120, 132l, 139 both, 142–143 both, 148c, 151r

Bennison Fabrics Ltd
16 Holbein Place
London SW1W 8NL
+44 (0)20 7730 8076
www.bennisonfabrics.com
pages 20a, 144–145

Bexon Woodhouse Creative
+44 (0)1531 630176
www.bexonwoodhouse.com
pages 8, 22

Binny Mathews
www.hereasel.com
Binny's portrait commissioning website
+44 (0)1935 83455
Stuart Martin
stuart@stuartmartinarchitects.com
01935 83543
Page 123l

Boonshill Farm B&B
Near Rye
East Sussex
www.boonshillfarm.co.uk
pages 58, 61r, 68–69, 87 both, 141, 148l

C

Christina Wilson
www.christinawilson.co.uk
page 115

D

Dandy Star
+44 (0)20 7923 7208
mail@dandystar.com
www.dandystar.com
page 78ar

Design By Us
www.design-by-us.com
also summer house in the South of France to rent:
www.villalagachon.com
pages 12–13, 53

Doris Urquhart and Christopher Richardson antiques
+44 (0)7799 414505
page 88l

E

Elizabeth Baer Textiles
+44 (0)1225 866136
dbaer@onetel.com
www.elizabethbaertextiles.com
page 51r

Elizabeth Machin Interiors PR
+44 (0)20 7503 3200
info@elizabethmachinpr.com
www.elizabethmachinpr.com
pages 16al, 117ar

Emma Bridgewater
739 Fulham Road
London SW6 5UL
+44 (0)20 7371 5489

www.emmabridgewater.co.uk
page 33l

Eva Johnson
www.evajohnson.com
pages 148–149

F

Fil de Fer
St.Kongensgade 83 A
1264 Copenhagen K
Denmark
+45 33 32 32 46
fildefer@fildefer.dk
www.fildefer.dk
pages 103r

G

Girl's Own Store
30 South Street
Bridport
Dorset DT6 3NQ
+44 (0)1308 424474
www.girlsownstore.co.uk
page 95r both

Gong
172 Fulham Road
London SW10 9PR
+44 (0)20 7370 7176
www.gong.co.uk
page 36l

Gustavo Martinez Design
27 West 96th Street
Suite 10F
New York, NY 10025
+ 1 212 686 3102
gmdecor@aol.com
www.gustavomartinezdesign.com
page 114al

H

Haberfield Hall
available for hire as a photographic location via:
Shootspaces
+44 (0)20 7912 9989
www.shootspaces.com
page 97

Heather Gratton
info@2refresh.com
www.2refresh.com
page 105

Helen Ellery
www.i-love-home.co.uk
page 93

I

i gigi General Store Ltd
31a Western Road
Hove
East Sussex BN3 1AF
+44 (0)1273 775257
igigi@igigigeneralstore.com
www.igigigeneralstore.com
pages 49, 100l

Ilaria Miani
Shop
Via Monserrato 35
00186 Roma
+39 0668 33160
ilariamiani@tin.it
www.ilariamiani.it
Podere Buon Riposo in Val d'Orcia
available to rent
page 128l

J

Jan Constantine
+44 (0)1270 821194
www.janconstantine.com
page 67

Jane Cumberbatch
www.purestyleonline.com
page 70

Jette Arendal Winther
www.arendal-ceramics.com
Pages 109r

John Pearse
6 Meard Street
London W1F OEG
+44 (0)20 7434 0738
jp@johnpearse .co.uk
www.johnpearse.co.uk
page 17

Josephine Macrander
+31 6 43053062
page 88r

Julian Stair
52a Hindmans Raod
London SE22 9NG
+44 (0)20 8693 4877
studio@julianstair.com
www.julianstair.com
page 24

K

Kate Forman
www.kateforman.co.uk
pages 28r, 32, 34r, 71l, 72c, 77l, 92r

Kathy Bruml Homestyle
+ 1 212 645 1241

kathy@kathybruml.com
www.kathybruml.com
page 107r

Kristiina Ratia Designs
+203 852 0027
pages 47, 132r

L

La Cour Beaudeval Antiquities
Mireille and Jean Claude Lothon
4 Rue Fontaines
28210 Faverolles
France
+ 33 2 37 51 47 67
pages 50, 51l, 72l

Le Clos du Léthé
Guest house – cooking classes
Hameau de St Médiers
30700 Montaren & St.Médiers
info@closdulethe.com
www.closdulethe.com
+33 4 66 74 58 37
page 23br

Lovelylovely
+44 (0)7989 645208
info@lovelylovely.net
www.lovelylovely.co.uk
page 96 both

M

Marianne Pascal Architecte D.P.L.G.
20 rue de l'Eglise 65700
Labout-Rivière
+33 6 35 21 17 84
www.mariannepascal.com
page 41

Michael Bains and Catherine Woram
www.catherineworam.co.uk
page 118l

Michael Leva
P.O. Box 100
Roxbury, CT 06783
USA
+1 860 355 2225
pages 140

N

Nina Hartmann
www.vintagebynina.com
pages 28l, 29, 52br, 103l, 128r, 138

O

Ole Lynggaard Copenhagen
Hellerupvej 15B
DK - 2900 Hellerup
+45 39 46 03 00
www.olelynggaard.dk
pages 11, 137

P

P + P Interiors
+44 (0)7956 404565
parkerminor@aol.com
pages 84, 114b

Penny Radford
Prato di Sotto
Santa Giuliana
Pierantonio (PG)
Italy 06015
+39 075 941 73 83
pennyradford@libero.it
www.umbriaholidays.com
page 45l

Petra Boase
info@petraboase.com
www.petraboase.com
page 124l

Philip Wagner Architects
5 Ladbroke Road
London W11 3PA
+44 (0)20 7221 3219
mailbox@philipwagner.co.uk
www.philipwagner.co.uk
page 89

Pour Quoi
Nodre Frihavnsgade 13
2100 Copenhagen
Denmark
+45 35 26 62 54
page 21

R

Raffaella Barker
info@locationpartnership.com
www.locationpartnership.com
property number HC601
page 134

Roger Oates
www.rogeroates.com
page 16br

S

Sanne Hjermind
artist
+45 26 91 01 97
Claes Bech-Poulsen
photographer
+45 40 19 93 99
claes@claesbp.com
www.claesbp.dk
pages 94–95

**Sasha Waddell Interior Design
& Lectures**
info@sashawaddelldesign.com
www.sashawaddelldesign.com
Sasha Waddell Furniture

+44 (0)20 8979 9189
www.sashawaddell.co.uk
pages 4, 9, 112–113, 132l

Space Architecture and Design
+45 35 24 84 84
mail@spacecph.dk
www.spacecph.dk
page 63

Stella Nova ApS
Blegdamsveg 28D, 2nd Floor
DK-2200 Copenahgen N
Denmark
+ 45 33 30 89 89
info@stella-nova.dk
www.stella-nova.dk
pages 100–101

Stephen Pardy
Weston Pardy Design Consultancy
49 Cleaver Square
London SE11.4EA
+44 (0)20 7587 0221
weston.pardy@mac.com
pages 110–111

Sue West
+44 (0)1453 757771
suewest@thehousemade.com
www.avaweb.co.uk/coachhouse.html
page 146

Susan Cropper
Loop
41 Cross Street
Islington
London N1 2BB
+44 (0)20 7288 1160
www.loopknitting.com
pages 52l, 117b

Swan House
1 Hill Street
Hastings TN34 3HU
+44 (0)1424 430014
res@swanhousehastings.co.uk
www.swanhousehastings.co.uk
No. Eight
www.noeight.co.uk
Melissa White
www.fairlyte.co.uk
pages 35, 112al, 121

T

Tapet Café
www.tapet-cafe.dk
pages 74l, 82ar

Teed Interiors Ltd.
for Sasha Waddell Fabrics & Furniture
www.sashawaddell.co.uk
pages 71ar, 77r

The Cross
141 Portland Road
London W11 4LR
+44 (0)20 7727 6760
pages 65l, 75

The Dodo
www.thedodo.co.uk
page 30l

The George in Rye
98 High Street
Rye
East Sussex TN31 7JT
+44 (0)1797 224114
stay@thegeorgeinrye.com
www.thegeorgeinrye.com
pages 64, 114ar, 118r

The Swedish Chair
+44 (0)20 8657 8560
www.theswedishchair.com
David Sandstrom, painter
murals and trompe d'oeil, painter
Sweden
+46 90 98049
pages 99r, 106–107

Todhunter Earle Interiors
+44 (0)20 7349 9999
interiors@todhunterearle.com
www.todhunterearle.com
page 40r, 83, 130

Twig Hutchinson
www.twighutchinson.com
pages 46l, 92l

V

Vivien Lawrence Interior Design
+44 (0)20 8209 0058/020 8209 0562
vl-interiordesign@cwcom.net
page 91r

W

Westcott Design Ltd
peter@westcott-design.com
www.westcott-design.com
+44 (0)20 7801 0072
page 123r

picture credits

Pages 1 *ph* Polly Wreford/Foster House, designed by Dave Coote & Atlanta Bartlett, available for photographic hire from www.beachstudios.co.uk; 2 *ph* Polly Wreford/Charlotte-Anne Fidler's home in London; 3 *ph* Polly Wreford/Foster House, designed by Dave Coote & Atlanta Bartlett, available for photographic hire from www.beachstudios.co.uk; 4 *ph* Polly Wreford/Sasha Waddell's home available from www.beachstudios.co.uk; 5 *ph* Paul Massey/a house in île de Ré; 6 *ph* Chris Everard/Jeremy Hackett's house in London; 7 *ph* Tom Leighton; 8 *ph* Christopher Drake/Fiona & Woody Woodhouse's 16th century weatherboard cottage in Surrey designed by Bexon Woodhouse Creative; 9 *ph* Polly Wreford/Sasha Waddell's home available from www.beachstudios.co.uk; 10 *ph* Chris Tubbs/Matthew & Miranda Eden's home in Wiltshire; 11 *ph* Paul Massey/the home in Denmark of Charlotte Lynggaard, designer of Ole Lynggaard Copenhagen; 12–13 *ph* Paul Massey; 14 *ph* Lisa Cohen/Clara Baillie's house on the Isle of Wight; 16al *ph* Jan Baldwin/Elizabeth Machin's Norfolk cottage; 16bl *ph* Andrew Wood/Fay & Roger Oates' house in Ledbury; 16r *ph* Debi Treloar/the home of Patty Collister in London, owner of An Angel At My Table; 17 *ph* Winfried Heinze/Florence & John Pearse's apartment in London; 18 *ph* Polly Wreford/Foster House, designed by Dave Coote & Atlanta Bartlett, available for photographic hire from www.beachstudios.co.uk; 19l *ph* Catherine Gratwicke/owner of Adamczewski, Hélène Adamczewski's former home in Lewes; 19r *ph* Winfried Heinze/Trine and William Miller's home in London; 20a *ph* Chris Tubbs/the Norfolk home of Geoff & Gilly Newberry of Bennison Fabrics; 20b *ph* Jan Baldwin/Claire Haithwaite and Dean Maryon's home in Amsterdam; 21 *ph* Lisa Cohen/the home of Lars Wiberg of Pour Quoi in Copenhagen; 22 *ph* Claire Richardson/the home of Fiona and Woody Woodhouse in Herefordshire; 23l *ph* Polly Wreford/designed by Dave Coote & Atlanta Bartlett, www.beachstudios.co.uk; 23ar *ph* Chris Tubbs/Matthew & Miranda Eden's home in Wiltshire; 23br *ph* Claire Richardson/Le Clos du Lethe; 24 *ph* Debi Treloar/the home and studio of Julian Stair in London; 25 *ph* Chris Tubbs/Annabel Grey's Norfolk Cottage; 26 *ph* Polly Wreford/Mary Foley's house in Connecticut; 27l *ph* Lisa Cohen; 27c *ph* Christopher Drake/Anna Bonde and artist Arne Tengblad's home in the Lubéron Valley, Provençe; 27r *ph* Polly Wreford/Foster House, designed by Dave Coote & Atlanta Bartlett, available for photographic hire from www.beachstudios.co.uk; 28r *ph* Lisa Cohen/Kate Forman's home; 28l & 29 *ph* Lisa Cohen/the designer Nina Hartmann's home in Sweden, www.vintagebynina.com; 30l *ph* Paul Massey/the Barton's seaside home in West Sussex: www.thedodo.co.uk; 30–31 *ph* Polly Wreford/Foster House, designed by Dave Coote & Atlanta Bartlett, available for photographic hire from www.beachstudios.co.uk; 32 *ph* Lisa Cohen/Kate Forman's home; 33l *ph* Chris Everard/a family home in Norfolk; 33ar *ph* Jan Baldwin; 33br *ph* Winfried Heinze/Trine and William Miller's home in London; 34l *ph* Caroline Arber; 34r *ph* Lisa Cohen/Kate Forman's home; 35 *ph* Claire Richardson/Swan House Bed & Breakfast in Hastings; 36l *ph* Polly Wreford/Jo Plismy, Gong; 36c *ph* Sandra Lane; 36–37 *ph* Polly Wreford/Stansfield Road designed by Dave Coote and Atlanta Bartlett, available for photographic hire from www.beachstudios.co.uk; 38al *ph* Polly Eltes; 38bl *ph* Dan Duchars; 38r *ph* Polly Wreford; 39 *ph* Lisa Cohen; 40l *ph* Polly Wreford/www.francescamills.com; 40r *ph* Chris Tubbs/designer Emily Todhunter's holiday home in the Peak District; 41 *ph* Winfried Heinze/a

Parisian pied-a-terre designed by Marianne Pascal for an Anglo-French couple; 42 *ph* Sandra Lane; 43l *ph* Polly Wreford/Mary Foley's house in Connecticut; 43r *ph* Chris Tubbs/Annabel Grey's Norfolk Cottage; 44 *ph* Jan Baldwin/Jan Hashey and Yasuo Minagawa; 45l *ph* Chris Tubbs/Prato di Sotto in Umbria designed and restored by Penny Radford; 45ar *ph* Peter Cassidy; 45br *ph* Caroline Arber; 46l *ph* Polly Wreford/the home of stylist Twig Hutchinson in London; 46r *ph* Thomas Stewart; 47 *ph* Debi Treloar/Kristiina Ratia and Jeff Gocke's family home in Norwalk, Connecticut; 48l *ph* Debi Treloar/Clare and David Mannix-Andrews' house, Hove, East Sussex; 48r *ph* Debi Treloar/Mark Chalmers' apartment in Amsterdam; 49 *ph* Polly Wreford/the home of Zoe Ellison, the owner of i gigi General Store in Hove, Sussex; 50 & 51l *ph* Christopher Drake/owners of La Cour Beaudeval Antiquities, Mireille and Jean Claude Lothon's house in Faverolles; 51r *ph* Chris Tubbs/Elizabeth Baer's early Georgian home; 52l *ph* Debi Treloar/Susan Cropper's former home in London; 52ar *ph* Lisa Cohen/Clara Baillie's house on the Isle of Wight; 52br *ph* Lisa Cohen/the designer Nina Hartmann's home in Sweden, www.vintagebynina.com; 53 *ph* Paul Massey; 54 *ph* Debi Treloar/Mark & Sally Bailey's home in Herefordshire; 55 *ph* Polly Wreford/Stansfield Road designed by Dave Coote and Atlanta Bartlett, available for photographic hire from www.beachstudios.co.uk; 56 *ph* Dan Duchars/stylist Rose Hammick and architect Andrew Treverton's former home in London; 57l *ph* James Merrell; 57c *ph* Debi Treloar/the home of Patty Collister in London, owner of An Angel At My Table; 57r *ph* Polly Wreford; 58 *ph* Polly Wreford/designer Lisette Pleasance and Mick Shaw's home/Boonshill Farm B&B; 59 *ph* Lisa Cohen; 60 *ph* Jan Baldwin/Jane Moran's cottage in Sussex; 61l *ph* Debi Treloar; 61r *ph* Polly Wreford/designer Lisette Pleasance and Mick Shaw's home/Boonshill Farm B&B; 62l *ph* Debi Treloar; 62r *ph* Dan Duchars/stylist Rose Hammick and architect Andrew Treverton's former home in London; 63 *ph* William Heinze/Signe Bindslev Henriksen of Space Architecture and Design; 64 *ph* Polly Wreford/the family home of Katie & Alex Clarke, the owners of the boutique hotel The George in Rye; 65l *ph* Debi Treloar/the home of Sarah O'Keefe, co-owner of 'The Cross' in West London; 65r *ph* Caroline Arber; 66l *ph* Winfried Heinze/Trine and William Miller's home in London; 66ar *ph* Debi Treloar/Bailey's Home and Garden; 66br *ph* James Merrell; 67 *ph* Paul Massey/Jan Constantine-www.janconstantine.com; 68–69 *ph* Polly Wreford/designer Lisette Pleasance and Mick Shaw's home/Boonshill Farm B&B; 70 *ph* Lisa Cohen/Jane Cumberbatch- www.purestyleonline.com; 71l *ph* Lisa Cohen/Kate Forman's home; 71ar *ph* Lisa Cohen/the designer Clare Teed's home in Hampton, www.sashawaddell.com; 71br *ph* Lisa Cohen; 72l *ph* Christopher Drake/owners of La Cour Beaudeval Antiquities, Mireille and Jean Claude Lothon's house in Faverolles; 72c *ph* Lisa Cohen/Kate Forman's home; 72–73 *ph* Debi Treloar/the home of Patty Collister in London, owner of An Angel At My Table; 74l *ph* Lisa Cohen/owner of TAPET-CAFÉ, Textile Designer Helene Blanche and husband and Jannik Martensen-Larsen; 74r *ph* Lisa Cohen; 75 *ph* Debi Treloar/the London home of Sam Robinson, co-owner of 'The Cross' and 'Cross the Road'; 76 *ph* Lisa Cohen; 77l *ph* Lisa Cohen/Kate Forman's home; 77c *ph* Polly Wreford/Foster House, designed by Dave Coote & Atlanta Bartlett, available for photographic hire from www.beachstudios.co.uk; 77r *ph* Lisa Cohen/the designer Clare Teed's home in Hampton, www.sashawaddell.com; 78l *ph* Paul Massey/Michael Giannelli & Greg Shano's home in East Hampton; 78ar *ph* Jan Baldwin/Rose Bamford

Dandy Star's home in Cornwall; **78b** *ph* Polly Wreford; **79** *ph* Polly Wreford/ Foster House, designed by Dave Coote & Atlanta Bartlett, available for photographic hire from www.beachstudios.co.uk; **80** *ph* Chris Tubbs/ Annabel Grey's Norfolk Cottage; **81** *ph* Polly Wreford/Stansfield Road designed by Dave Coote and Atlanta Bartlett, available for photographic hire from www.beachstudios.co.uk; **82al & b** *ph* Polly Wreford/Foster House, designed by Dave Coote & Atlanta Bartlett, available for photographic hire from www.beachstudios.co.uk; **82ar** *ph* Lisa Cohen/owner of TAPET-CAFÉ, Textile Designer Helene Blanche and husband and Jannik Martensen-Larsen; **83** *ph* Chris Tubbs/designer Emily Todhunter's holiday home in the Peak District; **84** *ph* Polly Wreford/Anna Parker, P + P Interiors; **86** *ph* Paul Massey/Michael Giannelli & Greg Shano's home in East Hampton; **87** both *ph* Polly Wreford/designer Lisette Pleasance and Mick Shaw's home/ Boonshill Farm B&B; **88l** *ph* Jan Baldwin/Doris Urquhart and Christopher Richardson; **88r** *ph* Debi Treloar/Wim and Josephine's apartment in Amsterdam; **89** *ph* Jan Baldwin/Philip & Lisskulla Wagner's cottage in Sussex designed by Philip Wagner Architects; **90–91** *ph* Polly Wreford/Foster House, designed by Dave Coote & Atlanta Bartlett, available for photographic hire from www.beachstudios.co.uk; **91r** *ph* Christopher Drake/Vivien Lawrence an interior designer in London (020 8209 0562); **92l** *ph* Polly Wreford/the home of stylist Twig Hutchinson in London; **92r** *ph* Lisa Cohen/ Kate Forman's home; **93** *ph* Chris Everard/a house in London designed by Helen Ellery; **94–95** *ph* Debi Treloar/Sanne Hjermind and Claes Bech-Poulsen; **95r** both *ph* Jan Baldwin/owner of Girl's Own Store, Sara Mahon's cottage in West Dorset; **96** both *ph* Debi Treloar/the London home of Louise Scott-Smith of www.lovelylovely.co.uk; **97** *ph* Debi Treloar/the home of Isobel Trenouth, her husband and their four children; **98** *ph* Debi Treloar/Mark & Sally Bailey's home in Herefordshire; **99l** *ph* Polly Wreford/Glenn Carwithen & Sue Miller, London; **99r** *ph* Debi Treloar/the Swedish Chair - Lena Renkel Eriksson; **100l** *ph* Polly Wreford/the home of Zoe Ellison, the owner of i gigi General Store in Hove, Sussex; **100–101** *ph* Winfried Heinze/the home of Kamilla Bryiel and Christian Permin in Copenhagen; **102** *ph* Lisa Cohen; **103l** *ph* Lisa Cohen/the designer Nina Hartmann's home in Sweden, www. vintagebynina.com; **103r** *ph* Winfried Heinze/the apartment of Lars Kristensen owner of Fil de Fer, Copenhagen; **104al** *ph* Chris Tubbs; **104ar** *ph* Polly Wreford; **104b** *ph* Chris Tubbs; **105** *ph* Polly Wreford/the Brighton home of Heather Gratton; **106–7** *ph* Debi Treloar/the Swedish Chair - Lena Renkel Eriksson; **107r** *ph* Polly Wreford/Kathy Bruml's home in New Jersey; **108l** *ph* Polly Wreford/Adria Ellis' apartment in New York; **108r** *ph* a family home in Lydd, Kent; **109l** *ph* Debi Treloar/ceramicist Jette Arendal Winther's home in Denmark, www.arendal-ceramics.com; **110–111** *ph* Christopher Drake/designer Stephen Pardy's Georgian house in London; **111r** *ph* Debi Treloar/Nicky Phillips' apartment in London; **112al** *ph* Claire Richardson/ Swan House Bed & Breakfast in Hastings; **112bl** *ph* Dan Duchars/stylist Rose Hammick and architect Andrew Treverton's former home in London; **112–113** *ph* Polly Wreford/Sasha Waddell's home available from www. beachstudios.co.uk; **114al** *ph* Debi Treloar/a family home in Manhattan, designed by architect Amanda Martocchio and Gustavo Martinez Design; **114ar** *ph* Polly Wreford/the family home of Katie & Alex Clarke, the owners of the boutique hotel The George in Rye; **114b** *ph* Polly Wreford/Anna Parker, P + P Interiors; **115** *ph* Chris Everard/Robert Elms and Christina Wilson's family home in London light courtesy of SCP; **116** *ph* Polly Wreford/Foster House,

designed by Dave Coote & Atlanta Bartlett, available for photographic hire from www.beachstudios.co.uk; **117al** *ph* Sandra Lane/the home of Patty Collister in London, owner of An Angel At My Table; **117ar** *ph* Jan Baldwin/ Elizabeth Machin's Norfolk cottage; **117b** *ph* Debi Treloar/Susan Cropper's former home in London; **118l** *ph* Polly Wreford/London home of Michael Bains and Catherine Woram; **118r** *ph* Polly Wreford/the family home of Katie & Alex Clarke, the owners of the boutique hotel The George in Rye; **119** *ph* Paul Massey/Michael Giannelli & Greg Shano's home in East Hampton; **120** *ph* Polly Wreford/Foster House, designed by Dave Coote & Atlanta Bartlett, available for photographic hire from www.beachstudios.co.uk; **121** *ph* Claire Richardson/Swan House Bed & Breakfast in Hastings; **122** *ph* Lisa Cohen; **123l** *ph* Jan Baldwin/artist Binny Mathews and architect Stuart Martin's home in Dorset; **123r** *ph* Jan Baldwin/owner of Westcott Design, Peter Westcott's cottage in Somerset; **124l** *ph* Debi Treloar/designer Petra Boase & family's home in Norfolk; **124r & 125** *ph* Claire Richardson; **126–127** *ph* Polly Wreford/Hilary Robertson and Alistair McGowan, Hastings; **127** *ph* Chris Tubbs/Marina Ferrara Pignatelli's home in Val d'Orcia, Tuscany; **128l** *ph* Chris Tubbs/Ilaria & Giorgio Miani's Podere Buon Riposo in Val d'Orcia; **128r** *ph* Lisa Cohen/the designer Nina Hartmann's home in Sweden, www. vintagebynina.com; **129** *ph* Paul Massey/Michael Giannelli & Greg Shano's home in East Hampton; **130** *ph* Chris Tubbs/designer Emily Todhunter's holiday home in the Peak District; **131a** *ph* Chris Everard/Jeremy Hackett's house in London; **131b** *ph* Debi Treloar/Nicky Phillips' apartment in London; **132l** *ph* Polly Wreford/Sasha Waddell's home available from www. beachstudios.co.uk; **132r** *ph* Debi Treloar/Kristiina Ratia and Jeff Gocke's family home in Norwalk, Connecticut; **133** *ph* Lisa Cohen; **134** *ph* Chris Tubbs/Raffaella Barker's house in Norfolk; **135al** *ph* Polly Wreford; **135ac** *ph* Debi Treloar; **135ar** Jan Baldwin; **135b** *ph* David Brittain; **136** *ph* Polly Wreford/Marina Coriasco; **137** *ph* Paul Massey/the home in Denmark of Charlotte Lynggaard, designer of Ole Lynggaard Copenhagen; **138** *ph* Lisa Cohen/the designer Nina Hartmann's home in Sweden, www.vintagebynina. com; **139** both *ph* Polly Wreford/Foster House, designed by Dave Coote & Atlanta Bartlett, available for photographic hire from www.beachstudios. co.uk; **140** *ph* Debi Treloar/Michael Leva's home in Litchfield County, Connecticut; **141** *ph* Polly Wreford/designer Lisette Pleasance and Mick Shaw's home/Boonshill Farm B&B; **142–143** both *ph* Polly Wreford/Foster House, designed by Dave Coote & Atlanta Bartlett, available for photographic hire from www.beachstudios.co.uk; **144l** *ph* Tom Leighton/Arne Maynard; **144–145** *ph* Chris Tubbs/the Norfolk home of Geoff & Gilly Newberry of Bennison Fabrics; **146** *ph* Catherine Gratwicke/interior designer Sue West's house in Gloucestershire; **147l** *ph* Lisa Cohen/Clara Baillie's house on the Isle of Wight; **147r** *ph* Polly Wreford/www.francesca mills.com; **148l** *ph* Polly Wreford/designer Lisette Pleasance and Mick Shaw's home/Boonshill Farm B&B; **148c** *ph* Polly Wreford/Foster House, designed by Dave Coote & Atlanta Bartlett, available for photographic hire from www.beachstudios.co.uk; **148–149** *ph* Christopher Drake/Eva Johnson's house in Suffolk, interiors designed by Eva Johnson; **150** *ph* Paul Massey/Michael Giannelli & Greg Shano's home in East Hampton; **151l** *ph* Lisa Cohen/Clara Baillie's house on the Isle of Wight; **151r** *ph* Polly Wreford/Foster House, designed by Dave Coote & Atlanta Bartlett, available for photographic hire from www.beachstudios. co.uk; **front cover** *ph* Ben Edwards; **back cover** *ph* Polly Wreford.

acknowledgments

This was a book that was very much after my own heart and it was indeed a joy to work with a team who understood so clearly and comprehensively what was needed in terms of both concept and realization. Thank you so much, Alison Starling and Leslie Harrington, Delphine Lawrance, Toni Kay and Emily Westlake.